SpringerBriefs in Environmental
Development and Peace

Volume 6

Series Editor

Hans Günter Brauch

For further volumes:
http://www.springer.com/series/10357
http://www.afes-press-books.de/html/SpringerBriefs_ESDP.htm

Lourdes Arizpe · Cristina Amescua
Editors

Anthropological Perspectives on Intangible Cultural Heritage

Organización : Cátedra UNESCO de Investigación
de las Naciones Unidas : sobre Patrimonio Cultural Intangible
para la Educación, : y Diversidad Cultural
la Ciencia y la Cultura : Universidad Nacional Autónoma de México

Editors
Lourdes Arizpe
Cristina Amescua
Centro Regional de Investigaciones
Universidad Nacional Autónoma de México
Cuernavaca
Morelos
Mexico

The cover photograph shows Chinelos at Yautepec's Carnival (2009). The photograph was taken by Rocío Hidalgo and is here reproduced with the permission of the photographer.

ISSN 2193-3162   ISSN 2193-3170   (electronic)
ISBN 978-3-319-00854-7   ISBN 978-3-319-00855-4   (eBook)
DOI 10.1007/978-3-319-00855-4
Springer Cham Heidelberg New York Dordrecht London

Library of Congress Control Number: 2013941533

Printed on acid-free paper

Springer is part of Springer Science+Business Media (www.springer.com)

Books by the Same Author Published by Springer

Lourdes Arizpe: *A Mexican Pioneer in Anthropology*. Springer Briefs on Pioneers in Science and Practice No. 10 – presented by Margarita Velázquez Gutiérrez (Cham – Heidelberg – New York – Dordrecht – London: Springer-Verlag, 2013).

Lourdes Arizpe: *Migration, Women and Social Development: Key Issues*. Springer Briefs on Pioneers in Science and Practice No. 11. Subseries Texts and Protocols No. 5 (Cham – Heidelberg – New York – Dordrecht – London: Springer-Verlag, 2014).

Lourdes Arizpe: *Culture, Diversity and Heritage: Major Studies*. Springer Briefs on Pioneers in Science and Practice No. 12. Subseries Texts and Protocols No. 6 (Cham – Heidelberg – New York – Dordrecht – London: Springer-Verlag, 2014).

Lourdes Arizpe: *Beyond Culture: Conviviability and the Sustainable Transition*. SpringerBriefs in Environment, Security, Development and Peace, vol. 13 (Cham – Heidelberg – New York – Dordrecht – London: Springer-Verlag, 2014).

Photo 1: Chinelos at Yautepec's Carnival (2012). *Source*: Photo by Alejandro Hernández

Acknowledgments

The *Research Planning Meeting on Intangible Cultural Heritage*, where the first drafts of these chapters were presented, was made possible with the support of Dr. Margarita Velázquez Gutiérrez, Director of Centro Regional de Investigaciones Multidisciplinarias (CRIM)—National University of Mexico (UNAM) and the funding provided both by Dr. José Narro Robles, Rector of the UNAM, and the project PAPIIT IN303409-3. Both the meeting and this volume are part of the activities of the International Social Science Council's and the International Union of Anthropological and Ethnological Sciences' Commission on Intangible Cultural Heritage and the UNESCO Chair in Research on Intangible Cultural Heritage and Cultural Diversity.

We would like to thank all participants in the meeting, whose input was fundamental in generating dynamic and enriching conversations: Antonio Arantes, David Berliner, Carolina Buenbrostro, Christoph Brumann, Susana Cuevas, Kristin Kuutma, Antonio Machuca, Shigeyuki Miyata, Úrsula Oswald Spring, Mary Louise Pratt, Montserrat Rebollo, Renato Rosaldo, Erendira Serrano Oswald, Hilario Topete, and Rodolfo Uribe.

We would also like to specially acknowledge the generous work of Erendira Serrano, Carolina Buenrostro and Edith Pérez-Flores during the meeting and during the editing process of this volume. Our gratitude also goes to the anonymous peer reviewers whose suggestions were a great contribution to each chapter in this volume.

Finally, a last word of recognition for Shirley Murguia who took great care translating Antonio Machuca's chapter, to Hans Günter Brauch for copy-editing and to Mike Headon (Wales) for his careful language editing, to Johanna Schwarz and Agata Öelschläger at Springer in Heidelberg, and to the producers and lay-outer of this book at Springer in Chennai, India.

Contents

Abbreviations

APINA	Council of Wajãpi Villages
APIWATA	Association of Wajãpi Indigenous Peoples of the Amapari Triangle
BCE	Before Common Era
CBO	Community-Based Organization
CGEN	Genetic Heritage Management Council
CNPq	Scientific and Technological Development Council
CRESPIAL	Centro Regional para la Salvaguardia del Patrimonio Cultural Inmaterial de América Latina (Regional Center for the Safeguarding of Intangible Cultural Heritage of Latin America)
CRIM	Centro Regional de Investigaciones Multidisciplinarias (Regional Center for Multidisciplinary Research)
FUNAI	National Indian Foundation
FUNASA	National Health Foundation
ICH	Intangible Cultural Heritage
INAH	Instituto Nacional de Antropologia e Historía (National Institute of Anthropology and History)
IPHAN	Instituto de Patrimônio Histórico e Artístico Nacional (Institute of National Historical and Artistic Heritage)
ISSC	International Social Science Council
IUAES	International Union of Anthropological and Ethnological Sciences
NGO	Non-governmental Organization
PR	Public Relations
RP	Recovery Point
UNAM	Universidad Nacional Autónoma de México (National Autonomous University of Mexico)
UNAOC	United Nations Alliance of Civilizations
UNESCO	United Nations Educational, Scientific and Cultural Organization
UNITWIN	University Twinning and Networking Programme
VE	Video Engineer
WIPO	World Intellectual Property Organization

Photo 2: Chinelos at Yautepec's Carnival (2012). *Source*: Photo by Alejandro Hernández

Introduction

In the rapidly evolving international framework of cooperation on culture, new anthropological research is needed on *intangible cultural heritage* (ICH), particularly on the impact of work undertaken by the United Nations Educational, Scientific and Cultural Organization (UNESCO) in this field. Anthropologists and other social scientists collaborated closely, through the International Social Science Council (ISSC), in the preparatory work for the 2003 *Convention for the Safeguarding of Intangible Cultural Heritage*. However, subsequent work on the Convention did not call on independent scientific organizations to collaborate until 2010 with the change of statutes by the General Assembly of State Parties to the 2003 Convention. These changes encouraged closer collaboration with research centers and universities and in response to this initiative a new *Commission on Intangible Cultural Heritage* was created in 2011 in the *International Union of Anthropological and Ethnological Sciences* (IUAES) which is one of the member organizations of the *International Social Science Council* (ISSC).

The Commission has sponsored several meetings and consultations with anthropologists and researchers working in related areas and is open to the participation of all experts interested in this field. At present, the Commission is chaired by Lourdes Arizpe, with Antonio Arantes and Kristin Kuutma acting as co-chairs and Cristina Amescua as Secretary. The *Regional Center for Multidisciplinary Research* (CRIM) of the *National Autonomous University of Mexico* (UNAM) will be hosting the Secretariat of the Commission for the next three years.

This book includes the chapters and the Report of the First Planning Meeting of the Commission on Research on Intangible Cultural Heritage held at CRIM in Cuernavaca, Mexico on 24–28 February 2012. All the chapters presented at the meeting were based on fieldwork and/or direct involvement in issues of reconceptualizing and assessing the outcomes of policy actions on ICH. The Report, in the Annexe, summarizes the main points and the discussion of issues relating to ICH discussed at the meeting.

Photo 3: Chinelos at Yautepec's Carnival (2009). *Source*: Photo by Rogelio Cuellar

As the chapters in this volume show, it is a priority to take up new issues and themes for research related to intangible cultural heritage. This will be useful in fostering broader interest in this topic among research communities in many countries, especially developing countries, and in enhancing UNESCO's work on the 2003 Convention.

Cuernavaca, Mexico, January 2013   Lourdes Arizpe

Chapter 1
Concepts and Contingencies in Heritage Politics

Kristin Kuutma

The booming field of current heritage studies is complex, versatile, and often characterized by contradictory significance or interpretation, as claims for heritage can appear to be simultaneously uplifting and profoundly problematic[1]. In essence, heritage is a value-laden concept that can never assume a neutral ground of connotation. Heritage indicates a mode of cultural production with reformative significance. My discussion of cultural heritage focuses on the practices of arbitration and engineering in the context of cultural politics. I propose to investigate the framework of concepts and contingencies that situate emergent heritage regimes. To start with the semantics of the core terms presented in the title, the act of arbitration conveys the idea of giving an authoritative decision, of judging or deciding in case of a dispute; engineering, in turn, signifies the making or achieving or getting something through contrivance, implying thus invention and formulation. In the following paragraphs, I will observe some aspects of engineering and arbitration from an abstract perspective, via the lens of concepts and contingencies that have proven instrumental in shaping and situating the discussion of heritage regimes. This reflection on concepts draws from the anthropology of politics concerning the domain of cultural heritage and its emergent regimes of engineering and arbitration while exploring relations between the communities, the state, and international institutions, which are defined by the circumstance of globalization, postcolonial empowerment, cross-cultural relations, 'translation', and management of cultural heritage.

When criticizing the notion of authorized heritage discourse, Laurajane Smith contends that the ways in which we write, talk and think about heritage issues matter

[1] This is a work-in-progress version of an article published in *Heritage Regimes and the State*, Universitätsverlag Göttingen, 2012. Research for this work was supported by the EU through the European Regional Development Fund (the Centre of Excellence in Cultural Theory), and by the Estonian Science Foundation, Grant No. 7795.

K. Kuutma (✉)
University of Tartu, Ülikooli 16-211, Tartu, Estonia
e-mail: kristin.kuutma@ut.ee

L. Arizpe and C. Amescua (eds.), *Anthropological Perspectives on Intangible Cultural Heritage*, SpringerBriefs in Environment, Security, Development and Peace 6, DOI: 10.1007/978-3-319-00855-4_1, © The Author(s) 2013

a great deal: this discourse privileges some social actors while disengaging others from their active use of heritage (2006). Dissonance and intangibility form the core qualities that channel and guide the perception of the nature of heritage and its effects; this concerns fundamentally the domain of cultural rights. Heritage is about the regulation and negotiation of the multiplicity of meaning in the past, and it is about the arbitration or mediation of the cultural and social politics of identity, belonging and exclusion. Perhaps it would be appropriate to use here the concept 'ideo-logic' suggested by Marc Augé: to designate configurations that articulate both relations of power and relations of meaning (Augé and Colleyn 2006, p. 47).

1.1 Curative Concerns

Regardless of the commonly prevailing celebratory approach, the fundamental conceptualization of the phenomenon comprises negative emotions and painful experience—destruction and loss are constitutive of heritage. The discordant nature of heritage preservation becomes painfully revealed in the context of the veneration of archaeological sites: their identification as such is the result of modern Western scholarship and its process of knowledge production. The archaeologist Lynn Meskell (2002), who has analysed disciplinary as well as political approaches to the Taliban destruction of the Bamiyan Buddhas in Afghanistan, describes the destroyed Buddhist statues as a site of 'negative heritage'—for the Taliban the statues had to be jettisoned in the nation's construction of contemporary memory precisely because they symbolized their own exclusion from the international community. For the West the site represents a permanent scar, a reminder of intolerance and symbolic violence (Fig. 1.1).

It has been suggested that the mission of UNESCO—which was originally mandated to engage in a worldwide educational campaign aimed at preventing new destructive conflicts like those suffered in the first half of the twentieth century—is an experiment in social engineering on a global scale (Stoczkowski 2009, p. 7). Here is the curative concern and ambition from the very beginning, finding a more recent translation into new meta-narratives of redemption and global reconstruction in the context of heritage care (Rowlands and Butler 2007, p. 1). The concept of care emerges as a central theme in the discussion of conflict and preservation. Phenomenologically, caring for something or somebody is fraught with anxiety, for it is contingent on unpredictable future events. Heritage care takes the notion of caution out of the museum—the birthplace of cultural curation—and re-embeds it in personal life (Rowlands and Butler 2007, p. 2). The fundamentalist ideology of heritage preservationism derives from the modernist obsession with loss, although David Lowenthal pointed out nearly three decades ago that loss expressed in the form of a monumental past is a feature of the present (Lowenthal 1985). When discussing the basic tenets of UNESCO's doctrine of human diversity, Wiktor Stoczkowski proposes to call it a 'secular soteriology', referring to the doctrine of salvation but giving it an extended meaning of

Fig. 1.1 Research planning meeting on intangible cultural heritage, CRIM–UNAM (2012) Cuernavaca, Morelos. *Source* photo by Carolina Buenrostro

deliverance from not only spiritual evil but also from material, social, economic, psychological, demographic, intellectual, etc. evil (2009, p. 8). The multivalent connotation of the verbal noun of 'engineering' has inspired Ulf Hannerz (2006) in turn, who has claimed that UNESCO's strategies are a mode of 'cultural engineering' based on nation-state logics and global governance. Heritage emerges from the nexus of politics and power; it is a project of symbolic domination: heritage privileges and empowers an elitist narrative of place while dominant ideologies create specific place identities which reinforce support for particular state structures and related political ideologies (Graham et al. 2000, p. 37). In addition, it simultaneously correlates with economic concerns which conversely relate to poverty and deprivation when we think about cultural expressions and environments in marginal communities or less affluent non-Western settings or countries. Heritage maintains a deep and complicated relationship with poverty. Heritage regimes and mobilizations create new arenas for competing political and economic interests that seek to appropriate viable heritage resources.

1.2 Arbitration

Barbara Kirshenblatt-Gimblett has argued that heritage as a mode of cultural production emanates from a metacultural relationship—heritage is created through metacultural operations (Kirshenblatt-Gimblett 1998, 2004) which gear the analysis of cultural heritage towards the examination of sociopolitical and economic entanglements. Heritage is about identifying and managing, and defined by selection and ownership. The policies of cultural heritage reveal presumably conflicting individual, communal or state perspectives observable in the predicaments of appropriation, contested restitution or celebration. Property relations are ultimately social and political. The making of heritage does not just depend on conceptual valorization; value is added both to symbolic and to material resources (Kirshenblatt-Gimblett 2006). Cultural heritage has reformative and powerful organizational and economic significance. In addition, even if the heritage under consideration and identified is claimed to be intangible, the process involved assumes materiality and tangibility, whereas the converse is true, depending at which end one stands or observes. At the same time the metacultural is inevitably turned into or embraced by the cultural.

The claims for materiality or intangibility of heritage unravel into essential ambivalence. On the one hand, cultural heritage is more widely known to be about place; about the situated, material, aesthetic and experiential aspects of culture. The dominant perception of 'heritage' draws heavily from the Western European architectural and archaeological conservation and preservation practices that define it as material, monumental, good, aesthetic, and of universal value. On the other hand, a conceptual shift has occurred in the last decade that has legitimized the term 'intangible' to define cultural expressions and practices (storytelling, craftsmanship, rituals, etc.) with the aim of being universally inclusive in avoiding the references to social stratum or inferiority that are perceived to be present in terms like 'folklore', 'traditional', or 'popular culture', and which global cultural politics considers too delimiting or prescriptive. At the same time the historicity of heritage needs to be formalized through material symbolism, which makes the intangible and ephemeral into something that has material form, be it on paper, a book, an audiovisual recording, particular elements of a festival, or an archive. Nevertheless, Laurajane Smith (2006) has argued that in an epistemological sense, all heritage is intangible because of the value ascribed to it and its social impact. The concept of heritage is used to legitimize or make material the intangibilities of culture and human experience. In essence, polarization into tangible and intangible is organizational and political, largely applied in order to demarcate target spheres and areas of expertise; it is the institutional distinction inside heritage industries that needs the division between tangible and intangible heritage. The recent re-theorization of heritage not only as sites, places, performances or events, but rather as a social construction and cultural practice, draws attention to the process of heritage-making by applying and recognizing the social significance of objects and expressions. Heritage is a social construction, a result of the process of 'cultural work' where the creation of heritage is directed by the 'authorized heritage discourse' (Smith 2006).

The latter emanates from a close interconnectedness of relevant national institutions with international organizations such as UNESCO, which has distinguished between the three major areas of heritage through its legal instruments of conventions: cultural heritage, divided into tangible and intangible, and natural heritage. The major documents that focus on and provide impact for heritage and initiate heritage studies are the *Convention Concerning the Protection of the World Cultural and Natural Heritage,* adopted in 1972, and the *Convention for the Safeguarding of the Intangible Cultural Heritage*, adopted in 2003.

1.3 Engineering

An international convention is a mandatory (legal) instrument for the member states that they are invited to ratify; subsequently they are invited to follow the operational guidelines for implementing the prescription of the document. The UNESCO conventions call for signatory states to prepare inventories, and if entries to various lists are attained, this entails the presentation of a vast amount of descriptive material. In sum, they need to produce documentation, which poses a problem from the point of view of the reification of culture. Any documentation is a parallel act to previous collection practices and is complexly related to issues of ownership, while such practice concerns itself with and highlights the exceptional (even if the opposite is aspired to).

Regina Bendix (2009) has claimed that heritage nominations reflect small-scale power play with large-scale effects of moralizing and ennobling. She contends that regimes of quality control and evaluation are always present in the process of heritagization, which depends on the late modern competitive practices that correspond to and signify the tendencies of 'audit culture', thus labelled and studied in academia by Marilyn Strathern (2000).

Inventorying is by default an act of classification. But it has been claimed that classification is culturally biased, being in essence a Western concern and practice (Arantes 2009, p. 54). The conflict becomes particularly significant when observed from the perspective of the triangle of indigenous groups, issues of ownership, and state. For example, indigenous groups may not wish or allow their intellectual property or environmental knowledge to be registered, because once documented, its ownership may easily pass out of their hands (Napier 2002). Inventorying raises the problem of subjectivity and agency in relation to the state—who has the right to travel, to document, to preserve? For example, in Venezuela inventorying has been carried out by the army, which probably acts in this capacity as it is the only institution accorded such 'liberties' under the prevailing sociopolitical circumstances.

An exercise in identification and categorization of dynamic and vibrant forms of human expression and mental capacities, the making of inventories proves eventually to be a task that instigates heated debates between cultural administrators, policymakers and scholarly experts in the field, but also on a larger scale between different social and political systems as well as between representatives of different historical experience and administrative practices. The principles of management that favour clearly defined categories and tacit hierarchies here confront the scholarly perception of culture that resists fixation and favours the living practices negotiated by their carriers on a daily basis between tradition and innovation. Drawing up inventories is an ambivalent problem—it is a controversial identification and mapping of cultural phenomena, a defining of communities and their heritage. This is an intervention that generates hierarchies and complicates the position of marginalities. On the one hand, all research relies on some kind of stocktaking, even if only mental stocktaking. Historically, archives and museums function on the basis of making catalogues and lists of cultural elements, even though these may often represent extinct past practices. Yet such a historical overview of culture comes from long-term observation, from going deep into the field, and also from participating. In the case of inventories of living cultural practices, however, the dissecting of different elements into distinct compartments means that cultural phenomena are detached and fragmented into manageable units. Yet cultural planning and management relies inherently on clearly defined and categorized elements. Thus cultural research and cultural politics deviate in essence, although they are actually interdependent. Nevertheless, in the present world of integrated global existence and the continuous collapse of time and space (thanks to the technologies that affect the size and scope of interaction), cultural research and cultural politics are inherently interdependent.

The politics of representation and decision-making happens to favour particular social groups. Antonio Arantes has pointed out that more often than not, the construction of public policies serves the cause of the elites, while he defines two social spheres in society: the cultural communities and the preservation institutions (2009, p. 62). On the other hand—and particularly in the preservationist camp—hybridity continues to be regarded as a negative feature from the perspective of heritage politics. This aspect can create additional friction, for example if we consider Brazilian culture in general, where the overall richness of cultural phenomena and practices derives inherently from hybrid mixtures. It may eventually appear an impossible task to pin down and define the moment when 'a hybrid' begins, i.e. when or where a mixture, a combination, a blend, a cross-breeding commences.

The identification and the evaluation of cultural heritage are inevitably surrounded by contestation. Programmes for its preservation and safeguarding pertain simultaneously to the politics of inclusion and exclusion: about who matters, who is counted in, who defines. The veneration of heritage tends to overshadow social inequalities (Bendix 2000). Heritage politics is never neutral, it is all about a choice that is implicitly and explicitly dependent on a notion of purity, whereas it shuns the existence of hybridity and qualities related to it. Heritage is selected or appointed in a complex process that involves particular politics when different groups simultaneously select and promote their symbols (Klein 2006). Furthermore, the relationship between community and heritage need not always be good and comfortable (Smith and Waterton 2009). Communities are not homogeneous, nor is their heritage; disjunctions occur, while the heritage claimed may not be consensual. A lot of social experience and practice can be related to contrast and conflict; these lead to pain and suffering, as has been shown by studies on dissonant heritage (Tunbridge and Ashworth 1996). This reflects the complexities of how communities define and negotiate memory and identity, how they communicate and engage with each other. On the other hand, the whole concept of community has been criticized for its presumed universalist claim. The choice as to how we define community membership can have serious social, political and economic impacts on individuals and groups within the state.

The other angle of potential achievement and concurrent deprivation emerges from programmes of development—another mechanism tacitly dependent on cultural engineering and arbitration—that either neglect or manipulate culture, with the potential involvement of communities.

1.4 Universalism and Representation

Heritage is perceived as providing a special sense of communal belonging. Though communities are seen as natural organizations of the populace, they actually come into existence through a need to organize boundaries and to interact with the community's antithesis, e.g. the government (Bennett 1998, p. 201). This becomes apparent in the context of making cultural policies where local communities find an outlet in activism, and seek to create an operational mechanism that gives them agency in local cultural policies. Policy-making will then function and activate at the community level, depending on the inclusion (as well as exclusion) of community representatives. The claims for heritage involve policy-making embedded in the framing of culture and its history and expression, combining insider activism with outside interests that involve political gain.

The politics of heritage protection has been traditionally mobilized from a Euro-American platform based on the presumed universalism of 'World Heritage', the logic of which has widespread effects in international and localized settings (Meskell 2010, p. 196), and impinges on the notions of development, neo-liberalism, and governmentality. The ultimate beneficiary is then the state authorities who manage to showcase 'culture', but is also transnational tourism companies, and perhaps those who gain employment in the process, mostly via consumption through global tourism.

The concept of 'World Heritage' involves a universalist pretension combined with a complex, highly structured praxis, based on uniform criteria descending from global to local contexts, thus inadvertently endorsing a globalizing programme (Turtinen 2000). And yet its impact and reverberations are still most poignant at the local level. An international organization like UNESCO depends on the institutionalization and maintenance of elite power and expert knowledge, while experts often come from the ranks of economic elites.

The underpinning or paradigm of intangible cultural heritage presumably differs from 'world heritage' (that of monuments, architecture and natural sites), the 'intangible heritage' being an outcome of a cultural relativist perspective influenced by postmodernist trends. If World Heritage designates and promotes 'outstanding universal value', then, in turn, Intangible Cultural Heritage manifests 'representativeness' in the regulatory conventions of and aspiring nominations to the UNESCO listing systems. The concept of 'intangible cultural heritage' involves a reflexive approach which depends on the 'human factor', as the potential for heritage is assumed to be established by its 'bearer' (Bortolotto 2010, p. 98). We might refer here to the notion of 'grassroots globalization' suggested by Arjun Appadurai (2002) when such collaborative approaches to heritage are assumed.

However, the involvement of communities is predestined to be weakened by the national validation process necessary for heritage authorization in the UNESCO system. The United Nations' definition addresses only a 'state party'. To what extent would protecting or safeguarding mechanisms go beyond securing the interest of state parties, in order to be capable of addressing localized needs and delivering culturally appropriate safeguarding mechanisms?

In the field of heritage policy, authority is accorded to expert knowledge and precedence given to professional interventions that create in turn particular communities of interest, involving stakeholders and stewardship. The discursive impact of the concept and perception of cultural heritage paves the way for a battleground of celebration and contestation among those entangled in the process of heritage production. Frictions based on cultural competence appear, conflicts between conservationists and innovators, hierarchies of authority. To a certain extent, these are opposed by local communities who claim ownership of a particular cultural heritage, and by communities for whom reaffirmation of their sense of belonging matters and hence who participate in the process of heritage production.

1.5 Governmentality and Culture

When heritage increases the value of a community, it serves the interest of the state.

With this in mind, it seems inevitable to consider the notion of governmentality in relation to heritage. My work in the anthropology of politics suggests an investigation into the construction and modalities of legitimate authority. As Marc Augé has proposed, in institutionalized power relations one should study not only the rules but also the practices that may be seen to contravene the normative dimensions (Augé and Colleyn 2006, p. 49).

Cultural forms and activities are deployed by governments as part of social management programmes. There is obviously a gap between the government and the communities, defined by various forms of unevenness. The state—a structured and centralized political organization, a mode of grouping and controlling people—is mostly perceived as a source of administrative authority and control, and as a repressive force; it is the entry point for international funds and it exercises control over different kinds of resources. However, it would be better not to see the state simply as an apparatus of power, but to study the diversity of ways in which power is exercised, the mechanisms of domination and stratification, the extension of political networks, the hierarchy of central institutions, the configurations and articulations of authority. One should likewise investigate the mechanism of power distribution, while distinguishing with Max Weber between power and authority, authority implying a promulgated measure of legitimacy.

Political discourse about a nation state entails disjunctions and discontinuities that are embedded in the political distinctions between centre and periphery. Anna Tsing (1993) has investigated the emergence and design of status-ranked areas from the perspective of unevenness, in order to tease out the logic and mechanisms that construct this gap between the government and the people. In her analysis of the formation of state authority from the perspective of the periphery, Tsing argues the need to move beyond "classic Marxist or Weberian frameworks, in which the state is an instrument of class interests or bureaucratic rationalization", in order to indicate "the symbolic fields in which power and politics are constituted". Scholarly understanding of the state could move "beyond the apparatus of government to show how the magic and power of state are formed in everyday discursive practice" (1993, p. 24) With the term 'state', Tsing refers to "those aspects of the governing, administrative, and coercive apparatus that are experienced as external yet hegemonic". The perspective of the periphery helps her analyse the imposed quality of state authority, and how the categories of state rule are actualized in local politics. 'Village politics' contribute to making the state, but the formation of local communities begins with the subjective experience of being both outside the state and subject to state power. While making explicit the political distinctions between centre and periphery, Tsing points to a dilemma of marginality that implies simultaneous placement inside and outside the state. She proposes to expand analyses of "the working of the state to include the political negotiations of out-of-the-way people" (1993, p. 25). This lends me the framework to study negotiations with the state in creating local cultural politics. Inspired by Tsing's conclusion that official state categories do not have the quality of 'always already', I consider it meaningful to look at cultural politics not as 'always already', but as an emergent framework formed in the nexus of culture, management and community.

When regarding the perspective of the state, the implementation of the framework of 'culture' stands out as the prominent preference: 'culture' is endorsed at state level for its capacity to provide a relief in potential conflict situations; it serves the state as an alternative to those politics that might complicate the state's authority (Tsing 1993).

1.6 Cultural Management

Tony Bennett has argued that the field of culture is now increasingly governmentally organized and constructed (1998, p. 61). He investigates the relationship between culture and the social by analysing the organization of contemporary cultural life through the various levels of engagement in policy-making. He examines the triangle of community, culture and government, to bring out the potential tensions between indigenous community and government, where government is usually observed from the position of cultural critique with indignation, condemning it as external and impositional, and indifferent or antagonistic to the creative cultural life. Yet it is "precisely from within the practices of government that 'community' acquires this paradoxical value of something that is both to be nurtured into existence by government while at the same time standing opposed to it" (1998. p. 201).

Bennett reaffirms that policy is central to the constitution of culture (1998, p. 106). He has called it "a reformer's science" when drawing attention to the management of cultural resources in a way that goes along with the intention to reform ways of life, as part of active politics and the policy of culture in contemporary society (1998, p. 104). Among the reforming endeavours is situated heritage politics, guided by ambivalent relationships between culture and power, depending on the organizational frameworks and institutional spaces under observation, embedded in the condition of either self-determination or its absence. Bennett's discussion of cultural policy from the perspective of normative mechanism outlines the historical conception of legislative or reforming orientation to culture. He is particularly interested in the management of cultural resources and cultural maintenance and administrative requirements in multicultural policies in particular.

Bennett's contention for the vital significance of cultural politics stands in opposition to Zygmunt Baumann's view of culture as a spontaneous process devoid of an administrative or managerial centre. From Baumann's position of postmodernist critique, culture cannot be 'made' or 'remade' as an object of practice, but should be considered a reality in its own right and beyond control, being "mastered cognitively, as a meaning, and not practically, as a task" (Bennett 1998, p. 102). Bennett considers this position particularly erroneous in multicultural situations (with marginal, minority communities in a modern society without nationalist uniformity) and points to the necessity of legislative mechanisms to produce respectful and tolerant relationships of cross-cultural understanding (1998, p. 103). Concurring with Bennett's claim that such cross-cultural understanding does not emanate naturally from the postmodern condition, I highlight here an important reason for studying cultural politics and how it is applied, or manipulated, at the local or grassroots level. When stating that "we do not only interpret the world, we also shape it" (1998, p. 104), Bennett locates a task of cultural management in the effort to recognize dissimilar cultural values and to promote forms of exchange between them.

1.7 Situatedness and Particularities

To conclude, let me return to what constitutes a heritage regime and how to go about investigating it. The deconstruction of an international 'authorized heritage' regime seems an obvious, though easy, undertaking. But what kind of agency will be gained or lost as a result of such an academic exercise? What is the moral agenda of this investigation and critique? The descriptive explanatory attitude unavoidably continues to assume normative dimensions such as social criticism, political commitment, and utopian longings, and perhaps even the defence of treasured ideals.

Heritage is a project of ideology that is dependent on ambivalent temporal entanglements. Its conceptualization depends on modernity's sense that the present needs to re-forge links with a past that appears to be severed and lost in the changing world. Its value-laden nature alludes to preservation and celebration of past elements of a reified culture intended to manifest ethnicity, locality and history; and yet the cultural politics involved with heritage proposes to address the concerns of the present, possibly with a perspective on the future. However, like all terms in the discourse of culture, heritage is an abstraction, and what it signifies is subject to an interpretation and an evaluation that may fluctuate between positive and negative over time and space.

Keeping that in mind, my suggestion is to take the situated character of globalization seriously, including in the critical study of heritage regimes, despite their seemingly common mechanisms at an abstract level. While considering the contended perceptions of globalisms, Anna Tsing has emphasized that anthropologists should extend their study of communities as narrowly defined social spheres to a wider-ranging scope of (transnational) networks, social movements, state policies, etc. (2002, p. 472). Transnational and global networks and 'universal' tendencies need to be ethnographically studied to unravel encounters, trajectories and engagements. But these processes with their global implications should not be observed simply as cases of imposed hegemony or self-evident homogenization, because globalist phenomena include not only unification but also local cultural divergence (Tsing 2002, p. 477).

Richard Handler (2002) has contended that cultural processes (such as heritage curation) are inherently particular and particularizing, so it would be unjustified to expect the reverberations and effect of a global policy to function and produce similar results under different circumstances. An anthropological approach advocates an investigation that utilizes different perspectives, so that it could contribute to our understanding of the social world by complicating simplicities. This means that concrete cases would benefit from being studied from a multi-sited perspective (as suggested by George Marcus 1998) which analyses decision-making at various levels: international, national, and particularly local. The local level also needs to be studied and analysed as a multi-sited field.

The observation of communities would penetrate deeper if communities were investigated as particularities—different circumstances make them perceive and employ the emergent potential of recognized agency and the acknowledgement of their cultural rights differently. The claimed universality is criticized for equating with Western values and codes of behaviour, whereas critical studies suggest instead an enabling resolve in pluralist approaches (Messer 1997). It seems important not only to elucidate and examine negative experiences and the violation of rights, but also to define and investigate moments of empowerment, real instances of emergent agency, situations where subjective agents take part in grassroots policy-making. 'Universal' rights acquire meaning by being applied as local variations. Communities may find agency in different aspects of their local politics. Thus the carefully explored particularities should help us bring out the complexity of the detached universalism of criticizing an institutional regime.

Heritage, itself a late-modern European concept and cultural phenomenon, is most controversial and yet instrumental from the perspective of 'intangible cultural heritage' in the context of non-Western cultural politics—it carries a strong potential for the acquisition of sociopolitical capital as well as channels for economic resources.[2] Cultural heritage has started to play an important role in international culture-orientated politics—cultural traditions and suppressed history have become powerful tools for regions that were dominated in the past. But it involves an ambivalent implementation of the category of time, where the preservation and celebration of past elements of reified culture mentioned above are implemented by cultural politics in order to address the concerns of the present, perhaps with a view to the future. In its programme to empower local and indigenous groups or equip particular expressive forms with political resonance, the employment of the notion of 'cultural heritage' has the capacity to overshadow the complexities of history and politics.

The mapping and identification of 'intangible heritage' as the premise for formulating cultural politics concerning indigenous groups signifies a new phase for them of reformative modernity, where shared experience and practices are transformed into political assets in both local and global arenas. This process inevitably involves the codification of cultural practices into manageable symbols of representation and argumentation. In this context, lived elements of culture are subjected to the discursive impact of previous ethnographic research and the veneration of past repertoires. On the other hand, the project of maintaining intangible heritage at local, national, and possibly international levels denotes an intervention that generates, or re-shifts and complicates, explicit and implicit hierarchies in or for the communities involved. Consequently, culture defined as 'intangible heritage' will eventually appear to be 'in transit'—from lived expressive forms to codified symbols implemented in cultural policy-making, and mediated at national and international levels through various agencies and organizations. However, it is not just a process of outside manipulation, but a two-way street with responsive local representation and appropriation from within in producing cultural, political and also economic agency. I wish to argue that 'heritage' groups are not passive receivers of cultural policies but also actors who make choices in negotiating or rejecting the options available, including those of contradiction and dissent. In the global reconfiguration of 'heritage production' and universal programmes of controversial impact, it seems important to recognize the

---

[2] In Europe, 'intangible cultural heritage' and the related UNESCO programmes have stirred great interest mostly in Eastern, post-Soviet Europe—explained, perhaps, by their relative political marginalization in comparison to the West, but also by their significant historical experience of the manifestation of identity through pre-industrial practices of expressive culture (Kuutma 2009).

Fig. 1.2 Chinelos at Yautepec's carnival (2009). *Source* photo by Edith Pérez-Flores

enabling conditions for particular instances. Even while concurring with the claim that 'the reification of tradition as culture entails its loss as social practice" (Herzfeld 1992), our research should be extended to observe the ways these 'reifications' function in the maintenance of cultural selfhood (Fig. 1.2).

References

Appadurai, Arjun, 2002: "Grassroots Globalization and the Research Imagination", in: Vincent, Joan (Ed.): *The Anthropology of Politics: A Reader in Ethnography, Theory and Critique* (Malden–Oxford: Blackwell Publishers): 271–284. .

Arantes, Antonio A., 2009: "Heritage as Culture: Limits, Uses and Implications of Intangible Cultural Heritage Inventories", in: Kono, Toshiyuki (Ed.): *Intangible Cultural Heritage and Intellectual Property: Communities, Cultural Diversity and Sustainable Development* (Antwerp–Oxford–Portland: Intersentia): 51–75.

Augé, Marc; Colleyn, Jean-Paul, 2006: *The World of the Anthropologist* (Oxford–New York: Berg).

Bendix, Regina, 2009: "Heritage between economy and politics: An assessment from the perspective of cultural anthropology", in: Smith, Laurajane; Akagawa, Natsuko (Eds.): *Intangible Heritage* (London–New York: Routledge).

Bendix, Regina, 2000: "Heredity, Hybridity and Heritage from One Fin de Siècle to the Next". in: Anttonen, Pertti J. (in collaboration with Siikala, Anna-Leena; Mathisen, Stein R.; Magnusson, Leif) (Eds.): *Folklore, Heritage Politics and Ethnic Diversity* (Sweden: Multicultural Centre): 37–54.

Bennett, Tony, 1998: *Culture: A Reformer's Science* (London–Thousand Oaks–New Delhi: Sage Publications).

Bortolotto, Chiara, 2010: "Globalising intangible cultural heritage? Between international arenas and local appropriations", in: Labadi, Sophia; Long, Colin (Eds.): *Heritage and Globalisation* (London–New York: Routledge): 97–114.

Graham, Brian; Ashworth, Gregory J.; Tunbridge, John E. 2000: *A Geography of Heritage: Power, Culture and Economy* (London: Arnold).

Handler, Richard, 2002: "Comments on Masterpieces of Oral and Intangible Culture", in: *Current Anthropology*, 43,1: 144.

Hannerz, Ulf, 2006: "Cosmopolitanism", in: Vincent, Joan; Nugent, David (Eds.): *A Companion to the Anthropology of Politics* (Oxford: Blackwell): 69–85.

Herzfeld, Michael, 1992: *The Social Production of Indifference* (Chicago: University of Chicago Press).

Kirshenblatt-Gimblett, Barbara, 1998: "Destination Culture: Tourism, Museums, and Heritage" (Berkeley–Los Angeles–London: University of California Press).

Kirshenblatt-Gimblett, Barbara, 2004: "Intangible Heritage as Metacultural Production", in: *Museum International*, 56, 1–2: 52–65.

Kirshenblatt-Gimblett, Barbara, 2006: "World Heritage and Cultural Economics", in: Karp, Ivan; Kratz, Corinne (with Buntinx, Gustavo; Kirshenblatt-Gimblett, Barbara; Rassool, Ciraj; Szwaja, Lynn; Ybarra-Frausto, Tomás) (Eds.): *Museum Frictions: Public Cultures/Global Transformations* (Durham: Duke University Press): 161–202.

Klein, Barbro, 2006: "Cultural Heritage, the Swedish Folklife Sphere, and the Others", in: *Cultural Analysis*, 5: 57–80. at: http://socrates.berkeley.edu/~caforum/

Kuutma, Kristin, 2009: "Who Owns Our Songs: Authority of Heritage and Resources for Restitution", in: *Ethnologia Europaea*, 39, 2: 26–40.

Lowenthal, David, 1985: *The Past Is a Foreign Country* (Cambridge: Cambridge University Press).

Napier, A. David, 2002: "Our Own Way. On Anthropology and Intellectual Property", in: MacClancy, Jeremy (Ed.): *Exotic No More: Anthropology on the Front Lines* (Chicago–London: University of Chicago Press): 287–319.

Marcus, George E., 1998: *Ethnography through Thick and Thin* (Princeton, NJ: Princeton University Press).

Meskell, Lynn, 2002: "Negative Heritage and Past Mastering in Archaeology", in: *Anthropological Quarterly*, 75: 557–74.

Meskell, Lynn, 2010: "Conflict Heritage and Expert Failure", in: Labadi, Sophia; Long, Colin (Eds.): *Heritage and Globalisation* (London–New York: Routledge): 192–201.

Messer, Ellen, 1997: "Pluralist Approaches to Human Rights", in: *Journal of Anthropological Research*, 53: 293–315.

Rowlands, Mike; Butler, Beverly, 2007: "Conflict and heritage care", in: *Anthropology Today*, 23, 1: 1–2.

Smith, Laurajane, 2006: *Uses of Heritage* (London: Routledge).

Smith, Laurajane; Emma, Waterton, 2009: *Heritage, Communities and Archaeology* (London: Duckworth).

Stoczkowski, Wiktor, 2009: "UNESCO's doctrine of human diversity: A secular soteriology?" *Anthropology Today* 25,3: 7–11.

Strathern, Marilyn, 2000: "Introduction: new accountabilities", in: Marilyn, Strathern (Ed.): *Audit Cultures: Anthropological studies in accountability, ethics and the academy* (London–New York: Routledge): 1–18.

Tunbridge, John E; Gregory J, Ashworth, 1996: *Dissonant Heritage: The Management of the Past as a Resource of Conflict* (Chichester: J. Wiley).

Turtinen, Jan, 2000: Globalising Heritage: On UNESCO and the Transnational Construction of a World Heritage. *SCORE Rapportserie* 12 (Stockholm: Stockholm Centre for Organizational Research) <http://www.score.su.se/pdfs/2000–2012.pdf>.

Tsing, Anna, 2002: "Conclusion: The Global Situation", in: Jonathan, Xavier Inda; Renato, Rosaldo, (Ed.) *The Anthropology of Globalization: a reader* (Malden–Oxford–Carlton: Blackwell Publishing): 453–485.

Tsing, Anna, 1993: *In the Realm of the Diamond Queen* (Princeton: Princeton University Press).

Chapter 2
Singularity and Micro-Regional Strategies in Intangible Cultural Heritage

Lourdes Arizpe

2.1 Introduction

In his 2011 book *Anthropology Confronts the Problems of the Modern World*, Lévi-Strauss states that "... always and everywhere, scientific explanation is based on what may be termed good simplifications. Given this relationship, anthropology turns necessity into virtue" (2011: 21). Such simplifications are then, however, carefully analysed according to disciplinary theories and discursive metonymies. In contrast, the texts of international normative instruments must answer to a very wide range of types of discursive acts and political outlooks, to mention only the most important factor influencing international policy negotiations.

Over and above this complexity, any international convention must arrive at a consensus in a most succinct and prudent text. As everyone knows who has been involved in negotiating policy documents, each word in the resolution or convention is filtered through very intricate considerations of various forms of knowledge and forecasts of political outcomes. Putting an idea and a text up for scrutiny by representatives of governments and peoples, in fact, gives such policy texts an underlying richness and a political legitimacy that no other kind of document can claim. When such negotiations are thinned out, for many reasons, words and proposals lose reflexivity and their contradictions increasingly complicate operational practices.

One way of ensuring a constant renewal of concepts and operational strategies in international programmes has been to build spaces in which policymakers, societal agents and social scientists may contrast ideas, forward-looking strategies and assessments of current operations. Critical perspectives are necessary to

L. Arizpe (✉)
Centro Regional de Investigaciones Multidisciplinarias, Universidad Nacional Autónoma de México, Av Universidad s/n Circuito II, Campus UAEM, Col. Chamilpa CP 62210 Cuernavaca, MOR, Mexico
e-mail: la2012@correo.crim.unam.mx

L. Arizpe and C. Amescua (eds.), *Anthropological Perspectives on Intangible Cultural Heritage*, SpringerBriefs in Environment, Security, Development and Peace 6, DOI: 10.1007/978-3-319-00855-4_2, © The Author(s) 2013

promote diversity and to allow innovations to influence policy decisions and drive programmes forward instead of into protracted negotiations by particular interests.

In recent years, anthropology has developed its own critical perspective on intangible cultural heritage, with little or no dialogue with the UNESCO programme of the 2003 Convention for the protection of this heritage. The 2007 *International Convention for the Protection of Cultural and Natural Heritage* fostered close collaboration with scientific organizations and even helped create and strengthen many of them. Since 2002, however, the work of the 2003 *Convention for the Protection of Intangible Cultural Heritage* has been conducted without the collaboration of anthropologists or other specialists, in spite of the fact that in the nineties and until 2002, anthropologists were very active in providing the foundational concepts for the Convention. The *International Social Science Council*, working closely with the *International Union of Anthropological and Ethnological Sciences* and other member organizations, was also active in the evaluation of the dossiers for the initial *Programme of Masterpieces of Intangible and Oral Heritage*. However, in 2002 UNESCO government delegations decided that only anthropologists brought to the discussions by governments were to participate in the debates for the final text of the Convention and in the follow-up of the Convention. In this sense it could be said that government delegations wanted a 'deregulated' Convention. It was only at the 2010 General Assembly of State Parties to the Convention that its statutes were changed to encourage collaboration with independent research institutions in the working of the Convention. Accordingly, in December 2010 the Commission on Intangible Cultural Heritage was formally created within the International Union of Anthropological and Ethnological Sciences and was adopted at the *International Social Science Council* (ISSC) in Nagoya in December 2010. The chapters in this book were all presented at the First Research Planning Meeting of this Commission at the *National Autonomous University of Mexico* (UNAM) in February, 2012.[1] The Report of this Meeting summarizes a large number of issues which need to be taken up in anthropological research, both in the general field of heritage studies and in relation to the implementation of the Convention.

The renewal of this dialogue between independent researchers in the field of anthropology and other related sciences and the policy-making bodies of the International Convention for the Protection of Intangible Cultural Heritage is now a very urgent matter, so that the vitality of its concepts can be maintained and new paths sought to overcome the difficulties that have arisen in the conceptual definition and operational methodologies of the Convention.

---

[1] See at:<http://132.248.35.1/informe/Informe.pdf>.

2.1.1   Three Examples of Singularity or Plurality

In this chapter one of these main issues is taken up, that of establishing the cultural boundaries of cultural practices classified for inclusion in the national inventories, the Representative List, or other Lists of the Convention on Intangible Cultural Heritage. Each ritual, festivity, knowledge or skill, to name only a few of the possible cultural practices, must be, in a sense, considered singular, in order to be included. Most cultural practices, however, belong to specific cultural areas and so many similar practices may be found in neighbouring villages or in a micro-region. Anthropology must look deeper into the dynamics of why and how cultural practitioners in different villages decide to invent a new single cultural practice or to borrow, adapt or adopt a practice from other towns or villages. Also, as I hope this paper will make clear, we need a clearer understanding of the micro-regional strategies that cultural practitioners and stakeholders develop in setting up similar events in neighbouring villages.

The analysis will be based on the fieldwork we have conducted in the past seven years on intangible cultural heritage in Mexico.[2] Three examples will be mentioned in this chapter: the commemorative performances, 'Simulacros'—a nineteenth-century term—, of the War of Independence of Mexico; the Dance of the Chinelos; and the Representation of the 'Malinches'.[3] Villagers re-enact these narratives knowing full well that they are sharing and adapting a celebration but in each case according to their own cultural preferences, following their own discourse of belonging, memory and contemporary relevance. They understand, then, that they are performing 'representations of representations'. How far is all intangible cultural heritage a 'representation of representations'?

The three examples of celebrations in the micro-regions of the Sierra de Guerrero and the north-east of the state of Morelos will be examined in terms of their singularity in a larger micro-regional framework of plurality. Singularity, as dealt with in anthropological literature, has to do with the originality and uniqueness of a cultural practice. Fieldwork has shown that these intangible cultural heritage practices are performed on the basis of the same narrative, and yet, significantly, are deliberately set apart by introducing a 'contrast' that will make the practice in each village slightly different from other similar practices in the micro-region. Underlined by friendly and sometimes not so friendly rivalry towards neighbouring villages, these 'marks of contrast', as I will call them, allow each group to construct a 'distinction', in the sense in which Bourdieu developed

---

[2] The project on intangible cultural heritage began in 2004 at the Center for Multidisciplinary Studies of the National University of Mexico, and since 2010 has been conducted in the framework of a Unesco–Unitwin Chair on Research on Intangible Cultural Heritage and Cultural Diversity.

[3] The word 'Malinche' comes from the Aztec (Nahuatl) *Malintzin*, originally used by Indians to refer to Hernan Cortes, the Spanish army commander, who had a native woman, Malintzin, translate native languages for him. The term then shifted towards the real Malintzin but became a pejorative term, synonymous with betrayal and, more recently, with anti-Mexican sentiments.

this concept. These 'marks of contrast' allow a group or a village to feel they belong to their larger cultural circle while at the same time maintaining their singularity.

The issue of singularity is closely related to that of authenticity. I will argue in this chapter that the problem of authenticity in intangible cultural heritage cannot be solved by isolating a single form of performance of a given practice since this would require an infinite listing of its historical, political, social, artistic and symbolic ontology. Instead, I propose that authenticity always be examined in the framework of the strategies of singularity and plurality of a cultural heritage practice. It is this framework that provides a template for the deliberate marking out by each group, village or town of their specific cultural event. This would make it easier to evaluate candidatures for inventories of the Convention Lists. It often happens that two groups or communities claim the origin or ownership of an event, and sometimes two or more countries may do so.

Pluriculturality is also a theme that can be found in at least two of the celebrations: the Dance of the Malinches in Tlacotepec and the Dance of the Chinelos in Yautepec. Local cultural practitioners have assembled their celebration by bringing together elements of several cultural traditions: the pre-Hispanic Meso-American cultures, Mexican mestizo culture, and Spanish and European traditions. This issue, however, will not be taken up in this chapter.

Attention will be paid to unfolding the dynamics of singularity-plurality on to geographical space so as to understand how the cultural practices that were studied are managed on a micro-regional basis.

2.2 Anthropology and Global Frameworks

The recent surge of interest in intangible cultural heritage may create new possibilities both for safeguarding existing living heritage and for constructing a new cosmopolitan vision of the ongoing transformation of such heritage in settings that none of us could even imagine a few decades ago. This is creating interesting new trends in knowledge and culture. As always, Claude Lévi-Strauss, in a recent lecture in Japan, expressed this way of understanding the plurality of world cultures:

> ...since the Western type of civilization no longer finds in its own resources that which would allow it to regenerate and take off towards a new flourishing, may it learn something...from those humble and, for a long time, disdained societies which, until recently, had escaped its influence? These are the questions that are being posed, after several decades, by thinkers, scholars and men of action and which incites them—since the other social sciences, more focused on the contemporary world, do not provide an answer—to interrogate anthropology (Lévi-Strauss 2011: 17).

Indeed, after two decades of a deconstructive transformation of its perspectives, anthropology is once again poised to make a vital contribution to the construction of a globalized cultural world. Anthropology seems to be coming out into the world again, as shown by many papers at the *Anthropology in the World* conference held at the British Museum in June 2012. The foundational 'global' viewpoint of anthropology, encompassing all human societies around the world, is an idea whose time has gradually become more relevant, as the world becomes more 'global' and, more to the point, as sustainability creates an imperative to work for all humanity. More specifically, anthropology's global ambition and its exact knowledge of microspheres, of local groups and places, is now urgently needed to reassess a process of maldevelopment and globalization that has created extremes of wealth and access, of exclusion and violence.

Interestingly, while anthropologists have been highly critical of many of the foundational concepts of their discipline—including the concepts of 'culture', 'civilization', 'community', 'indigenous' and so on—it is highly significant that recent political ideologies, for example in the discursive form of 'multiculturalism' or the 'clash of civilizations', have not hesitated to reify culture and to revive many of the terms that anthropology had discarded precisely because they obscure, rather than illuminate, cultural processes.

2.2.1 Anthropology and Intangible Cultural Heritage Programmes

Locating anthropology's interest in cultural heritage no longer in the framework of seeking universals in ethnological patterns of human organization but in the current debate about globalizing human communications, economic exchanges and political allegiances provides a very rich soil in which to ground research. Cultural heritage is studied in anthropology not only because of its evolutionary or intercultural salience but mainly because of its importance to current negotiations on remaining 'human', protecting vulnerable peoples, defending cultural identities, linking culture to development and finding effective paths towards sustainability. That is, anthropology is dealing with new social forms of intersubjective relations.

Given these themes, it is easier to understand the relationship of anthropological research to a cultural policy programme as specific as the safeguarding of intangible cultural heritage. Although studies of physical cultural heritage have developed rapidly in the last four decades through archaeology, architecture, anthropology and museology, this was not the case with the living heritage of indigenous and mixed peoples.

Since the eighties anthropology, and especially interpretive anthropology and ethnomethodology, have influenced the 'cultural turn' of critical and postmodern studies with attention shifting towards meanings, signs and symbols. This new emphasis was brought to UNESCO just at the time—in the nineties—when the culture sector was beginning a new round of consultations, on the one hand to link development and culture, and on the other to develop an international convention on intangible cultural heritage.[4]

To put it simply, new perspectives and initiatives on culture were mushrooming around the world as globalization spread. The United Nations Commission on Culture and Development was able to tap into these in its nine consultations around the world for its report *Our Creative Diversity* published in 1996. To illustrate the diversity of viewpoints at the time, it is worth including a few of the major statements given at these consultations by artists, indigenous peoples, cultural activists and government cultural policy officials.

On the very first day of the meeting of the Commission, Claude Ake asked pointedly why wars of culture had increased at that time. Cultures, he explained, are not developed or underdeveloped; ethnic conflicts arise as a result of non-development. Yet, he warned, there also exists a culture of hatred, of discrimination, of fascism, "so it's not a question of bringing in culture in a good way". Comments came from Mahbub ul Haq: "… future conflicts will not be between nations but between peoples and nations…"; from Ase Kleveland: "… just as the culture of democracy seems to spread, the governability of our societies appears to decline … it is clearly unacceptable, whatever our cultural background is, in world income distribution, that the richest receive eighty per cent of world income and the poorest twenty per cent only 1.4 %"; from Alaine Touraine: "while the global market is in the hands of the North, identities are in the South … we need political reason against tribes and the market"; from Edith Sizoo: "… isn't culture behind separatism, racism, machismo, the burning of widows, the mutilation of sexual organs? … a key problem is that actions and interventions are carried out in a power relation that determines whether things will change"; from Fernando Calderon: "… conflicts which prevailed in the sphere of production have now been transferred to the sphere of culture … [some voices are now suggesting] a way to overcome the dialectics of exclusion by living individual identity, belonging to a community and engaging in productive modernization"; from Roberto Da Matta: "… what are, then, the sources of national identity? Rituals. In Brazil, the classical components of the bourgeoisie have been lost but instead, there is popular music, the carnival, they give a sense of place and identity"; from Yao Jie Hou: "… the culture of ancient civilizations continues to influence their development and culture is an entire system of spiritual and social values"; from Kapila Vatsayanan, who referred to the Asian, African and Meso-American cultures: "… the only contrast among such civilizations is with post-Renaissance Europe and this is the difference of thinking in terms of man and Nature and not man in Nature. This makes for a very different understanding of what the self is, of what a human being is in the matrix of the natural world"; from Mamadou Dia: "… indigenous institutions are limited, they have women and age discrimination; and transplanted ones as well. So even with investments we have not had good results. So we went to the other side, to the 'fundamentalist tradition' institutions, to romanticization. So now we need renovated indigenous institutions

---

[4] The author was Assistant Director-General for Culture at UNESCO 1994–1998.

and converging transplanted institutions". Ms Werewere Liking commented: "… it is the practitioners of culture that should be in the forefront. We have had segmentation due to apartheid. … Every person has the right and possibility of creating culture. It is also being shaped by the man chiselling a mask in his backyard", and the Director of the South African Museum "… in Africa cultural actions are much more important than cultural buildings, we have life inside us, which we share with others".

The point in citing these statements is that they gave us members of the Commission a much nuanced view of the possibilities of focusing national and international policies on new guidelines for the safeguarding of the diversity of world cultures. The Report of the Commission established the background for many of the international cultural initiatives taken by UNESCO and its member states at the beginning of the new century.

2.2.2 A New Concern for Living Cultures

As mentioned, concern for the safeguarding of living cultures began with the adoption of the International Convention for the Protection of the Natural and Cultural Heritage in 1972. By the nineties, demands for 'cultural survival' and the protection of living cultures seemed to come from everywhere: from government delegates and diplomats at the United Nations; from anthropologists concerned with the cultural survival of small-scale societies; from the rising movements of indigenous and autochthonous peoples; from artists and performers; from Ministries of Culture in very different countries. All were confronted not just by the impact of globalization and the market economy but very markedly by the rapid expansion of the media and telecommunications, films and videos.

By now there was also a different perception of cultural policies among the governments of developing countries. At a very memorable meeting of the Executive Board of UNESCO in Fez, Morocco in 1995, delegation after delegation, especially from developing countries, asked for a new direction in UNESCO's cultural policy. Just a few months earlier, at a meeting in Nara, Japan, the criteria for the World Heritage List had been thoroughly reviewed and changed. Now, member states insisted on having greater attention given to 'living heritage' so that historic centres in cities would not become silent, so that peoples' living cultures should not only be put behind glass panes in museums but rather that local neighbourhoods and villages could be active participants in safeguarding their cultural heritage.

A new, initial programme was set up, the programme on Masterpieces of Oral and Intangible Cultural Heritage which was the forerunner to the Convention. At the time, following the traditional way in which UNESCO programmes operated, the dossiers for the candidatures of the Masterpieces Programme were relayed to

the International Social Science Council.[5] Through its scientific member organizations, the Council then distributed the proposals to anthropologists and other
social scientists around the world who had specific knowledge of the cultural
groups in the regions involved, for a technical assessment.

As mentioned earlier, this collaboration between international scientific organizations and the work of the Convention ceased when UNESCO government
delegations decided that all scientific knowledge and cultural expertise would be
filtered exclusively through government delegations in negotiating the Convention
and making it operational. Consequently, no independent anthropological research,
no systematic examination of the outcomes of inscriptions on the Lists of the 2003
Convention, and no reaching out towards new knowledge that was being developed in universities, museums and many other cultural institutions were brought in
so as to refresh the thinking and management of the Convention. In some countries, such as Mexico, the selection of candidatures for the Representative List
became over-politicized, leading to a multiplicity of experimental forms of
decision-making in the work of the Convention and, more disquieting still, the
proliferation of many kinds of intermediaries who, in some cases, have swept aside
or manipulated cultural practitioners as the major actors of the Convention.

Debates based on philosophical and scientific knowledge, in my experience, by
their very nature bring in a diversity of interpretations that enlarge the spaces for
negotiation and for finding the exact conceptual nuances to slowly work towards
consensus. Without such debates, content becomes empty and debates drag on
bitterly and mainly on the basis of immediate political interests. Most importantly,
scientific endorsement gives a legitimacy which is tied to historical and larger
political concerns that help keep checks and balances between politics and
institutions.

For all the above reasons, it is very important that anthropology engages in
rigorous study of intangible cultural heritage, both to bring clarity to its concepts
and interpretations but, most importantly, to support, through in-depth knowledge,
the development of new ways of understanding and organizing fluid identities and
cultural claims in a liquid and effervescing second modernity. Most centrally for
this paper, the engagement of anthropologists and other social scientists is vital to
maintain the checks and balances that will give agency to cultural practitioners in
the work of the Convention.

2.3 "We Will Continue to Celebrate Here"

In contributing to understanding the dynamics of the singularity and plurality of
cultural practices, anthropology is also very important in insisting on the flowing
nature of culture, so that cultural fundamentalisms leading to violent conflicts may

---

[5] At that time, this author was President of the International Social Science Council.

be stemmed. In the UNESCO World Culture report of 2001 (UNESCO 2001), we argued that reifying cultures into hardened, discrete units was not only far from reality but unhelpful in setting up policy-oriented programmes. Instead, we proposed that cultures be understood as 'Rainbow Rivers' in which, at different historical times, cultural practitioners either kept up separate and singular cultural traditions or mixed or blended their own cultures with the cultures of other groups. This cultural flow is one of the great challenges of the Convention, since a List, any list, entails carving the boundaries of specific cultural practices from their historic cultural tapestry.

In many countries, one of the issues creating heightened conflicts over intangible cultural heritage is the rivalry between different ethnic, cultural, religious and national groups in decisions about inventorying and presenting candidatures for the ICH Representative List. An ethnic group may claim as exclusively its own a certain dance or cultural practice while another or several others may also lay claim to it. It is clear that cultural proximity, syncretism, hybridity and imitation of cultural practices, all inherent characteristics of cultural evolution, inevitably limit the right that one group may have over others in proposing their representations as candidatures and in receiving the exposure and privilege that inclusion in the List is now bringing. While historical and anthropological data and research may assist in clarifying questions of cultural boundaries, a much more complex model is needed to explain the dynamics of cultural borrowings or exchanges. A complex methodological question is: how can the singularity of a given cultural practice be mapped out, in local and micro-regional terms, so that all neighbouring representations are given proper recognition? What happens when two or more villages claim to be the site of origin of a celebration?

A key remark was made by Eugenio Navarro, a young man in the town of Acatempan. He explained that for many, many decades, they have celebrated the 'Abrazo de Acatempan'—the 'Embrace of Acatempan'—in his village, with the participation of a neighbouring town, Teloloapan. This event in Mexican history commemorates the purported meeting in 1820 between the General of the Insurgents (those who fought for Mexican independence from Spain), General Vicente Guerrero, and General Agustin de Iturbide, who had formerly belonged to the Royalist Army of the King of Spain but who now switched sides to fight with the Insurgents. The historical evidence for this meeting is shaky and there is another town of Acatempan in a neighbouring state which also claims that the meeting took place there. Amid the doubts and claims, Eugenio Navarro, the young man in Acatempan in the state of Guerrero (the name was taken from General Guerrero) told us flatly, "… some historians say that the meeting did not take place here, that it was elsewhere, but we don't care. We have been celebrating this meeting here for more than a hundred years and we will continue to do so."

When questioned further, Eugenio explained that this allows them to have friendly discussions with people in the neighbouring town of Teloloapan, where they organize the group that comes with General Iturbide. Dressed in full regimental garb, General Iturbide and his soldiers, all on horseback, come to meet with General Guerrero and his group of cavaliers, who have been riding all over the hills surrounding Acatempan. Riders take three letters between the Generals. After meeting in a plaza filled with people of both places, and a long dialogue—written, they say, in the nineteenth century—with both protagonists showing off their prowess as cavalrymen, the two Generals embrace, joining their two armies and ensuring that Mexican independence was then rapidly achieved.

When I asked another older woman in Acatempan why they held this celebration with the people of Teloloapan, she said shyly, "Well, it is much better this way, they don't fight so much". "Who fights?" I asked. And she murmured, "It's because they are hacendados (in this context 'rich landowners') over there. Here, we're Indians, so it is better this way". This example, as did others during the fieldwork, indicates that the dynamics of celebrations in towns and villages are marked by the previous historic relationships between such neighbouring towns and villages. Such 'civic intangible cultural heritage' is seen as a way of maintaining peaceful and friendly relations between different communities (Figs. 2.1, 2.2, 2.3, 2.4 and 2.5).

I have also termed this civic cultural heritage 'social capital' because several informants in that and other villages mentioned that holding these large celebrations was a way of keeping young men off the streets and off drink, and of having young men and women participating in the celebration meeting and having fun. As such local celebrations wane, the loss of cooperative mingling leaves young people in empty spaces, where they are easily swept up by the drug traffickers and criminal organizations.

In this micro-region, as well as in others where I did fieldwork, local people said that they are very keen on their own celebration—or that of any other of their fiestas, for that matter—being well appreciated by people coming from other localities in the region. What makes the celebrations appreciated by neighbouring

Fig. 2.1 El Abrazo de Acatempan, Acatempan, Guerrero (2010). *Source* Photo by Edith Pérez-Flores

Fig. 2.2 Representation of Mexico's Independence, Chilacachapa, Guerrero (2009). *Source* Photo by Alejandro Hernández

cultural practitioners and stakeholders? Items mentioned in different villages vary but basically they refer to showing off the affluence of the village, which can be made ostentatious in the costumes, horses and artefacts used by the performers, in the copiousness of the meals offered freely at the villagers' houses for visitors from outside, in the abundance of free liquor and beer offered to the public, and in the beauty of the floral and other decorations at the sites where the celebration is held.

The voices heard as people disband after the performances are unequivocal in this respect: "...this year [the celebration] was a very sparkling display" ("Este año [la fiesta] salió muy lucida"); or, on the contrary, "...this year [the celebration] was very poor" ("Este año salió muy pobrecita"). The responsibility for the glitter or the opaqueness of the celebrations is in the hands of the organizers, whether the traditional 'majordomos' or the municipal authorities. Such is the importance of these celebrations that municipal governments are known to have been toppled because they held a very inadequate celebration.

Fig. 2.3 Representation of Mexico's Independence, Chilacachapa, Guerrero (2009). *Source* Photo by Alejandro Hernández

2.4 "We Do the Same, But Different"

Through fieldwork, with the team of young anthropologists working on the project to create an Archive of Intangible Cultural Heritage at the National University of Mexico, we discovered that in many rural communities in Mexico, they hold performances related to the War of Independence, as well as to the Mexican Revolution of 1910. The reason these celebrations had been overlooked in anthropological research is that they are neither wholly indigenous, nor official commemorations of the War of Independence. And I ask myself how much intangible cultural heritage has been overlooked because it does not fit neatly into the cultural classifications of general ethnographic grids applied in many countries.

In the eighteen communities (Arizpe 2011) in which we carried out fieldwork, the general discourse is based on the national historical narratives, yet, in each village, the organizers decide which scenes to highlight and which ones to leave out, thereby opening up spaces of contrast. In some villages they have an original text. For example, in Jantetelco the 'Comedy'—as theatre plays were called in Mexico in the nineteenth century—on the life of the one of the distinguished leaders of the War of Independence, Mariano Matamoros, was written in 1881 and is still performed today. In others, the celebration was recently invented, as in

Fig. 2.4 Chinelos of Tlayacapan at Yautepec's Carnival (2012). *Source* Photo by Carolina Buenrostro

Fig. 2.5 Dance of Las Malinches, Tlacotepec, Morelos (2008). *Source* Photo by Cristina Amescua

Tetelpa in 1943—and focuses only on the victory over Fort Alhondiga de Granaditas that was held by the Spaniards.

In yet other cases, the whole sequence of scenes of the War of Independence is performed during a great three-day event. In the latter case, in Chilacachapa, the local historian, Eusebio Ramirez, when asked why the same celebration was held in over seven neighbouring villages of the Sierra, explained "Yes, we are doing the same, but different" ("Si, hacemos lo mismo pero diferente"). Clearly, it seems to me, this is a case of cultural practitioners being aware that they are performing 'representations of representations' rewritten and resignified through their own agency.

Chilacachapa, a large village in the Sierra of Guerrero perched over the valley of the Rio Balsas which flows into the Pacific Ocean, holds an extraordinary three-day event involving some 120 young cultural practitioners and more than 3,000 stakeholders. I consider the latter stakeholders because they are not only an attentive audience but most of them contribute something to the event: a meal, some sweets, a bottle of drink; or they are directly involved in helping their daughter, son, niece, cousin or grandchild sew up their costumes. The scenes performed at various sites in the village are based on the historical narratives of Mexican independence, but the villagers are proud of the choices they have made as to the different kinds of scenes.

How do these celebrations vary? While the way the 'Simulacros' are organized in the villages depends on the specific conditions of each annual event such as the amount of money provided by the 'majordomos'—village-appointed heads of the celebration—authorities and stakeholders, the number of volunteers, especially young people, who want to participate, and the agreement of other villages near and far to bring their groups of dancers or performers, many other differences are deliberately introduced. People in the villages were constantly explaining what they did differently from the commemorations in other villages. For example, in Chilacachapa, Don Eusebio explained that "We don't build a big Alhondiga [Fort] here, but, instead, the party goes on for three days. Over there, it only goes on for one day" ("Aca no hacemos una Alhondiga grande pero, en cambio, aqui dura tres dias la fiesta. Allá [en Teloloapan] dura namas un dia").

In Chilacachapa, they have chosen to hold a skirmish—'escaramuza'—between Insurgent forces and the Spanish Royalist army in the evening of the first day, and a grand battle—'la Batalla'—the next day in the afternoon. There is also another 'small battle' held on a bridge on the second day at 6 a.m. They also enact the 'hanging' of the Royalists by tying a rope around the waists of the 'soldiers' and hoisting them over a pole. Young men and women have hilarious fun trying to pull them upwards when some of the 'soldiers' are quite stout men. Other villages do not perform the skirmish nor the 'hanging' of the Royalists nor the 'small battle' on the bridge. The people of Chilacachapa very proudly declare that their 'Simulacro' is the largest and best known of the celebrations among the seven others held in the neighbouring town and villages.

Another 'mark of contrast' of their celebrations is actually the day on which it is held and which I interpret as a micro-regional strategy. Although the national official date of Independence Day is 15 September, the Simulacro in Chilacachapa takes place on 8 October. When I asked why it is held on that date, it was explained me that in this way people from other villages could come to their celebration. Indeed, the celebration of Independence is held in the municipal town on 15 September; in Machito de las Flores on 28 September; in Apipilulco on 22–26 September, in Apetlanca on 18–20 October, and so on. This pattern is very similar to that of at least the Mexica (Aztec) empire in pre-Hispanic times. The larger town, *altepetl*, held the most important festivities and established the very profuse ritual calendar that allowed the smaller villages and barrios, *calpulli*, to hold their festivities consecutively. This micro-regional strategy allowed, as it does even today, every village the possibility of holding their own celebrations and market so that everyone else from neighbouring communities is able to attend.

2.4.1 Micro-Regional Strategies in the Dance of the Chinelos

A second example of a cultural practice which is carried out as singular event, yet it is included in the framework of a plurality of similar events, is that of the 'Jumping Chinelos' ('El Salto del Chinelo'). This dance is held in three different villages in the northern region of the state of Morelos, each with very marked contrasts in costumes, choreography, parades, and the gender participation and social diversity of its performers. The dance was invented, according to informants, at the beginning of the twentieth century, in the village of Tlayacapan. The dancers created a new mask, white with a pointed black beard, which, as they explain, represents the Spaniards. The original Tlayacapan Chinelo costume was a simple white gown embroidered with blue lace, and the headdress included, initially, vases of flowers and later faces and symbols, all embroidered with beads.

Several years later, in the same Tlahuica[6] micro-region, cultural practitioners in the neighbouring village of Tepoztlán also took up the Chinelo dance, and made it quite famous by including it in their annual town festival honouring *Ce Acatl Tepiltzin Quetzalcoatl*, a Meso-American historic and mythical figure, on 8 September. These practitioners say they made the costume 'more elegant' by using black velvet for the gown with colourful borders added, by embroidering more elaborate scenes in the headdress, and by wearing black, very pointed shoes. "Why?", I asked. "Because here we are different" ("Porque aqui somos diferentes") was the answer. Thus, while borrowing the Dance from Tlayacapan, they introduced 'marks of contrast' to create a cultural boundary.

The cultural practitioners of Yautepec went even further in establishing a contrast when they took up the Dance of the Chinelos. They readily accept that they also borrowed the general idea of the Dance and the costume from Tlayacapan, but they explain why they introduced many changes both in the costume of the Chinelo and in the way it is performed in Yautepec. The members of the

---

[6] 'Tlahuica' is the name given in some historic sources to the Nahua peoples of the northern part of the state of Morelos in some historic sources and has been used recently to establish a contrast between speakers of the Nahuatl language in the state of Morelos and those of the adjoining states of Mexico and of Puebla. Again, this is an example of the use of contrast to create a tenuous cultural boundary that reinforces a micro-regional identity.

'Cultural Group' organized to promote the Dance explained that the village of Yautepec was famous in pre-Hispanic Meso-America for its production of highly-valued textiles which were given as tribute to the Mexica (Aztec) Empire. So they decided to honour this tradition by introducing highly-skilled embroideries of pre-Hispanic historical scenes in the Chinelo gown and headdress.

Also in contrast to the other two villages, they inserted the Chinelo Dance into their Carnival festivities in the month of February along with various other parades. The fiesta starts with a Widow's Parade or the Parade against Bad Humour. It is a humorous parade of men dressed as women, who carry the dead husband, the Bad Humour, in a coffin that is then thrown into the river. The best-dressed and best-looking of them then participate in a beauty pageant. Although people in the town quickly explain that all these men are actually married, there is evidence that in Meso-American and North American pre-Columbian traditions homosexuals had an accepted role in society so it is highly probable that they also participated in festive parades. Many European Carnivals, though, also include what have been termed 'inversion' scenes or characters that exhibit out-of-the-norm ways of behaving.

In the recent initiative by a group of local people to establish a Museum of the Chinelo, they found evidence that women had been very active in creating the parade in Yautepec in 1935. This participation has continued, since women dress up as Chinelos for the parade. A few elderly women interviewed explained that they had been 'dancing' in the parade for more than forty years. This is in contrast to the festivities in Tlayacapan and Tepoztlan, where only men participate as Chinelos. Again, a mark of contrast.

Yautepec cultural practitioners recently innovated by holding a Chinelo children's parade in the morning on the day before the Carnival. "If they don't learn and then love it, then they won't participate in the parade later on." As it happens, at present, the main parade is also filled with young people. Some dress as Chinelos, but interestingly, creating their own generational marks of contrast, they participate in groups that practice the Capoeira, the Brazilian martial dance, Senegalese drum dances—a group in the region actually went to Senegal to refine their techniques—, and the Arab belly-dance. This aspect is very significant since it shows that, while people in Yautepec want to claim their own identity among the different Chinelo celebrations, they are very open to the participation by local practitioners of the cultural dances of other countries.

It is worth summarizing here the overlay of cultural traditions that went into creating the singular event of the Chinelo Dance in Yautepec. It may be called its 'cultural stratigraphy'. Firstly, as mentioned, Yautepecans borrowed the idea and costume of the Chinelo Dance from Yautepec, with additions from Tepoztlan which they also kept, thereby adhering to a micro-regional tradition of *plurality*. Secondly, they innovated by adding original applications of embroidered Meso-American depictions to the Chinelo costume, thereby establishing a 'mark of contrast' to highlight its *singularity*. Other marks of contrast are the participation of children and women and a gay parade. Thirdly, they allow the participation of groups of young women and men dancing international cultural traditions: in the framework of the European Carnival, they have made a cultural collage with African, Brazilian and Middle Eastern influences, thereby affirming that theirs is a *pluricultural* event. In sum, through their innovations to the Chinelo Dance, Yautepecans have both confirmed their belonging to a plural, micro-regional cultural tradition, and to a pluricultural world, while at the same time highlighting their singularity as a town that has a unique historical tradition to offer.

A very different but interesting point that may be raised here is that the scenes that are embroidered on the gowns are depictions taken from the National Museum of Anthropology and History in Mexico City and other historical and anthropological sources of intangible cultural heritage. This is clearly a case in which the reconstructions and representations constructed by historians, archaeologists and ethnologists bring back ancient traditions that today cultural practitioners proudly want to acknowledge. This flow of cultural knowledge was made possible because of the cultural policy sustained by the Mexican government throughout the twentieth century. Its main tenet was that culture, in general, is a public good. Hence the cultural policy that led to the building of exemplary museological, ethnographic, popular culture and educational cultural programmes in Mexico which influenced the cultural policies and programmes of other countries as well as the International Convention for the Protection of Cultural Heritage.[7] In recent years the 'right to culture' has been inserted into the Mexican constitution.

2.4.2 The Dance of the Malinches: A Pluricultural Celebration

A third example may help to clarify the issue of pluriculturality in intangible cultural heritage. This is the totally original event of the 'Danza de las Malinches' of Tlacotepec. Original in the sense that such an event was constructed by schoolteachers in rural villages in the 1930 by amalgamating both the indigenous and the Spanish cultural heritage, while giving it, in Tlacotepec, a very special contrast. The event begins with a performance of the literary 'Dialogue between America and Spain', a beautiful text written by Juan de Dios Peza, a Mexican writer from the end of the nineteenth century.

Two young women, one dressed as a Mexica (Aztec) princess, another as the Queen of Spain, recite this text that describes the beauties and bounties of America and Spain, ending with the reconciliation of both traditions. The Mexica princess is dressed in a satin robe with the national colours, green, white and red, and wears a

---

[7] The second UNESCO General Conference was held in 1948 in Mexico, where archaeological, ethnographic and educational cultural programmes were demonstrated. A year later, the Culture Sector of UNESCO was created. Mexican specialists were also very active in UNESCO's work on international conventions to protect cultural and intangible cultural heritage, as well as in other culture programs.

diadem with feathers, resembling the Meso-American headdress, indigenous sandals and arrows in a *carcaj* (quiver: container for arrows).

Then, the most ebullient part of the pageant unfolds. Four or five little girls dress up as *'inditas'*—an affectionate term for little Indian girls—, with a rein-vented costume that mixes local and regional indigenous elements: *'ixtle'* woven sandals (*'cacles'* in Nahuatl), black woollen wrap-around skirts, and Mexican ribbons and necklaces. While dancing, they sing a song which was originally meant to be in Nahuatl, the indigenous language which is still spoken in the region, but whose words can no longer be recognized as such. In the final scene, indig-enous baskets, *'chiquihuites'* (also Nahuatl), are brought on stage. This creates a great stir and expectancy in the audience, as the girls begin to throw out savoury tamales, a Mexican bread made of maize that people, especially young people and children, catch in the air with great joy.

The pluriculturality of this event has both visible and implicit references to different cultures. The art of declaiming and speaking 'beautifully' was a highly developed activity in the Mexica empire and most of Meso-America. It is even attested to in the pre-Hispanic Codices by the inverted comma that signals public speech and by the appreciation for 'flowery singing or speaking', 'flor y canto' ('in xochitl, in cuicatl' in Nahuatl). At the same time, public recitation was a much appreciated activity in Spanish culture, as was rhetoric. The colours, symbols and dress of the young women and girls reflect a representation of Spanish culture or of Mexica and contemporary indigenous cultures.

As the aim of the literary text of the Dialogue of America and Spain is precisely the reconciliation of both sides of the Mexican identity, the composition and performance of the event goes beyond the images, to underlying cultural mean-ings. The mark of contrast introduced by the people of Tlacotepec, since a similar kind of event also takes place in other communities of the micro-region, is the throwing of tamales to the public. This is a gesture of generosity and of sharing which is at the core of indigenous cultures in Mexico.

2.4.3 Conclusion

As a conclusion to this brief explanation of three types of practices of intangible cultural heritage, I would point out that the classificatory grid for intangible cul-tural heritage events must take into account these three dimensions: firstly, the singularity of an event, marked deliberately for contrast in the framework of a plurality of similar practices; secondly, the pluriculturality of the event must be signalled, simply stating the major cultural influences that it has received from other cultures; and, thirdly, attention must be given to micro-regional strategies that also allow communities to integrate into a single, ritual calendar which holds together their conception of time, unity and belonging.

Developing operational criteria to understand the reassembling of symbolic, social and political undercurrents is very important for the inclusion of cultural practices in the Lists of the International Convention on Intangible Cultural Heritage. It will also help in giving recognition to other groups having the same kinds of practices, and acknowledging histories of pluriculturality.

There have already been many conflicting claims about specific practices of intangible cultural heritage being presented for the Lists, which are becoming ever more complex as they begin to be couched in terms of intellectual property, a term that is still controversial. This issue becomes even more complicated when it is linked to the administrative and political scale of representation of such events.

2.5 Multiscalar Representations in Intangible Cultural Heritage

If one were to ask, which of the Chinelo Dances of Tlayacapan, Tepoztlan and Yautepec is the "authentic" one, it would be difficult to answer. To unfold the intricate narrative of the Yautepec Chinelo Dance, one would have to delve into the various criteria to be taken into account: who invented it? Did they actually authorize other copies of their Chinelo Dance? Who agreed to hold it in other villages? How were innovations introduced in the other two towns? All these questions of who and how, it must be said, would be considered totally absurd by local people. Why, because culture flows. For them the borrowing or offering is part of the natural order of things.

This is how intangible cultural heritage is perceived among most indigenous, autochthonous and local townspeople around the world. Hence the difficulties in pinning down types of cultural practices and especially their attributes. It would facilitate this task, however, if cultural performances were analysed as processes in which, at different times, events were highlighted because they are singular, plural or pluricultural; this would allow programmed activities to keep the natural flow that all intangible cultural practices have.

References

Arizpe, Lourdes (Ed.), 2011: *Compartir el Patrimonio Cultural Intangible: Narrativas y Representaciones* (México: Consejo Nacional para la Cultura y las Artes and Centro Regional de Investigaciones Multidisciplinarias).

Lévi-Strauss, Claude, 2011: *L'Anthropologie Face aux Problèmes du Monde Moderne* (Paris: Seuil).

UNESCO, 1996: *Report of the World Commission Culture and Development: Our Creative Diversity* (Paris: UNESCO).

UNESCO, 2001: *World Culture Report: Culture, Conflicts and Pluralism* (Paris: UNESCO).

Chapter 3
Evaluation of Items on Intangible Cultural Heritage

Renato Rosaldo

Evaluation is built into the notion of intangible heritage in a number of senses. Intangible heritage, in other words, is a normative concept. Intangible heritage is a relational term which is understood in contrast with tangible heritage. Intangible heritage is considered to be of less obvious value than the tangible. It is the immaterial or the ephemeral as opposed to the material or the enduring, even permanent. Tangible heritage, by contrast, is a monument, say, a cathedral or an aqueduct or a still-standing ancient city of exquisite beauty. In this relationship, the intangible appears less substantial, less enduring and hence of less obvious value (Fig. 3.1).

The claim to worth of intangible heritage is that of a vital, changing, yet long-lasting tradition of song or story, dance or cuisine, knowledge and skills involved in the production of material objects. With current technology for recording speech and body movement, much that is called intangible can be archived and studied and thus made part of the human record in ways that were not possible fifty years ago. The intangible can thus be an object of research.

One possible research project is: how does UNESCO determine which cultural practices are of sufficient value to be included in the list of items of intangible heritage? And, of course, how does UNESCO decide to exclude other items from its list? The animating question would be: by what processes are such evaluations of inclusion and exclusion determined? How, in practice, are these questions of relative value decided?

A second and perhaps more urgent research project could be to investigate how practitioners and their audiences evaluate the qualities of intangible heritage. What is the vocabulary of evaluation? What are the key native terms? What, more broadly, is the language of the determination of value? What, for example, according to the singers, makes one song better than another? If there are musicians: how do they make such evaluations? How do they evaluate one singing of

R. Rosaldo (✉)
New York University, Rufus D. Smith Hall, 25 Waverly Place, New York, NY 10003, USA
e-mail: renato.rosaldo@nyu.edu

L. Arizpe and C. Amescua (eds.), *Anthropological Perspectives on Intangible Cultural Heritage*, SpringerBriefs in Environment, Security, Development and Peace 6, DOI: 10.1007/978-3-319-00855-4_3, © The Author(s) 2013

Fig. 3.1 Renato Rosaldo (*red cap*) and Antonio Arantes (*black cap*) at Yautepec's Carnival (2012). *Source* Photo by Alejandro Hernández

one song versus another? How do singers evaluate their audiences? And how do audiences evaluate the singers? This inquiry could also compare different songs that are seen as related or somehow comparable.

Most ethnographic studies do not encompass such questions of value, yet these issues are eminently researchable. They might begin with simple questions of taste, such as which one somebody likes better, but their goal would be to explore the aesthetics of a community. How do such evaluations take place? Are they based on notions of beauty or utility or form or sacred power? Can such investigations determine how central certain items of intangible heritage are, or are not, to particular cultural formations?

Chapter 4
Beyond Tradition: Cultural Mediation in the Safeguarding of ICH

Antonio A. Arantes

Cultural preservation as a public policy is a product of Western cultural history which developed organically as part of the process of formation of nation states. Therefore, it can and should be the object of critical reflection. In relation to intangible goods, this development is more than 10 years old, in various countries as well as in the global public cultural sphere. This is not the place to conduct a critical review of the results achieved by national conservation bodies or by UNESCO, supported by active non-governmental organizations and academic specialists. But it is time to focus on a certain malaise that is often manifested in academic milieux around what is currently called 'patrimonialization', mainly when the cultural dynamics of heritage holder communities is at stake.

From this perspective, the aim of this chapter is to question how the ascription of *patrimonial value* affects local politics and interferes with the development of traditional knowledge and cultural expression. I will also make some suggestions about the role of mediators (or social brokers) in the negotiations that take place between government officials and cultural communities as part of the safeguarding process. My approach is based on the following premises:

(1) The identification of cultural elements that might be relevant from a patrimonial perspective is based on complex intercultural dialogues and negotiations.
(2) Inventories are necessarily selective. They highlight some cultural elements and understate others; give access to material and symbolic benefits to some

This chapter is based on "The problem: from the Wajãpi point of view", Chap. 2 of Arantes (2009), originally published by the *World Intellectual Property Organization* (WIPO) on its official website at http://www.wipo.int/tk/en/culturalheritage/surveys.html. The Secretariat of WIPO, copyright owner, assumes no liability or responsibility with regards to any transformation of this material.

A. A. Arantes (✉)
Universidade Estadual de Campinas, Rua Cora Coralina s/n—Cidade Universitária, "Zeferino Vaz", Barão Geraldo, Caixa-postal: 6110, Campinas-SP 13081-970, Brazil
e-mail: antonio_arantes@terra.com.br

L. Arizpe and C. Amescua (eds.), *Anthropological Perspectives on Intangible Cultural Heritage*, SpringerBriefs in Environment, Security, Development and Peace 6, DOI: 10.1007/978-3-319-00855-4_4, © The Author(s) 2013

activities and social groups, and exclude others, often generating within communities expectations that are not always fulfilled. Furthermore, they are usually conducted in circumstances that frequently do not contribute to reaching academically desirable levels of ethnographic density. They can therefore be grounded in doubtful interpretations about the cultural meanings enrooted in the social practices that they aim to nurture.

(3) Safeguarding can be interpreted as a mechanism through which the cultural elements of everyday life are assigned patrimonial value and so transformed into meta-cultural realities; in other words, they become official representations of current representations and practices. It follows from this that documentation, promotion and dissemination of such elements may be anthropologically interpreted as ways of *staging heritage* and therefore *enacting* the social identities and cultural differences that it represents.

On the basis of these premises, one could raise the following questions about the consequences of safeguarding: would it lead to shifting cultural elements from an authenticity/counterfeit axis to one that articulates historical verisimilitude with creations for the market, or with pure fantasy? If such is the case, would the final result of safeguarding contribute more to strengthening the tradition of cultural preservation rather than to actually nurturing current social practices? Or to feeding the market and the so-called creative industries with new ideas for new products?

In a critical reflection on safeguarding, the premises above place at the forefront the nature of the relationship between government agencies and ICH holders. Certainly, most—if not all—institutional regulations affirm that it is up to ICH producers and holders to decide whether they do or do not want to incorporate these agencies as partners in their own projects in safeguarding current cultural practices. There is no doubt about this, and it could be no other way. But to what extent do the parties involved—all of them—have clear ideas about the implications of the elements in play in these negotiations, whether from a legal perspective or from the point of view of local custom, economics and politics? How far can the consequences of safeguarding be anticipated and controlled?

These questions are pertinent to the present reflections because, in addition to choices of or preferences for political strategy, they involve deeper issues of a moral and cognitive nature. This is because certain categories and procedures that give structure to legal instruments do not necessarily find equivalents in the concepts and practices institutionalized by custom. I refer here to themes such as the segmentation of social experience in elements or domains, to the distinction between material and non-material aspects of social realities, to the idea of intellectual property, and so on.

Due to these differences, safeguarding is, to a large extent, the result of a process of cultural translation, which can be more or less efficient, depending on the conditions in which this dialogue takes place. There are cases in which ICH holders have community members who are qualified and politically organized in ways that make negotiations with government agencies viable. But very often the

ICH holders' worldviews and forms of organization are *not* compatible with the requirements of the state's bureaucracy. In these cases, establishing contacts, making and implementing decisions and evaluating results become extremely arduous tasks and their aims are not always achieved. In such cases non-governmental organizations, academic researchers and activists usually act as intermediaries. To confront these structural difficulties is an inescapable challenge for safeguarding policies. These are subjects on which perhaps only the rough and rugged ground of ethnographic experience can throw some light and it was with these concerns in mind that I conducted brief fieldwork among the Wajãpi people of Amapá.

The Wajãpi are the holders of the graphic language *kusiwa,* which was registered on 20 December 2002 in the *Livro de Registro das Formas de Expressão* [Registration Book of the Forms of Expression] by *Instituto de Patrimônio Histórico e Artístico Nacional* [Institute of National Historical and Artistic Heritage] (IPHAN) as an element of Brazilian Cultural Heritage. It was proclaimed—together with the corresponding orally transmitted knowledge—a Masterpiece of the Oral and Intangible Heritage of Humanity by UNESCO in 2003, and included in the ICH Representative List in 2008.

This fieldwork was part of a survey commissioned by the Creative Heritage Project set up by the World Intellectual Property Organization (WIPO)[1] to address the codes and guidelines used by archives, preservation institutions and researchers for making and disseminating audiovisual ethnographic registers of traditional knowledge and cultural expressions in Brazil. My decision to bring an indigenous perspective to the project[2] aimed to exemplify the sort of difficulties that traditional communities have when confronted with such demands. Now I intend to rethink the issue within a broader perspective, so as to contribute to a better understanding of the complex relations that the safeguarding process builds among the officials of preservation agencies and among ICH holders. My field observation aimed at understanding the Wajãpi's views on the following issues: Who owns the graphic expressions, festivals, songs and dances proclaimed as cultural heritage? How are these forms of knowledge acquired and transmitted? Are non-community members allowed to make audio and/or visual recordings of these practices and disseminate these registers? If yes, or if no, then why? Who makes this decision, how, and in whose name? If permission is granted, what limits are set and conditions established for such undertakings? If such permissions produce material benefits, how are these benefits shared?

---

[1] More information on the Creative Heritage Project can be found at <http://www.wipo.int/tk/en/culturalheritage>.

[2] I would like to express my sincere gratitude to the Wajãpi and to the Iepé staff for their support to this project and particularly to Dominique Tilkin Gallois, who has so generously shared her knowledge and experience. I would also like to thank WIPO, especially Wend Wendland and the Creative Heritage Project staff, for accepting the idea of including these fieldwork observations in our plans, despite the practical difficulties that this has entailed.

4.1 The Wajãpi of Amapá

The population self-denominated as Wajãpi lives in three locations on the border between Brazil and French Guyana and does not constitute a culturally homogeneous community. For the questions focused on in this study, the group of approximately 915 people (Pesquisadores Wajãpi 2008) who live in the forty-eight villages existing in the Wajãpi Indigenous Land is particularly relevant. Their territory was officially established in 1996 and is located in the central western region of the state of Amapá, encompassing 607,000 hectares. Following current usage in the official documents consulted (Gallois 2002, 2006, and others), this group is designated here as "the Wajãpi of Amapá".

My observation took place during a workshop for training indigenous researchers given by anthropologist Dominique Tilkin Gallois at the Aramirã Post. This is a regular activity of the Wajãpi Programme, created in 1992 by the non-governmental organization (NGO) Iepé Institute.[3] Besides informal observation, participation in activities of everyday life at the village and interaction with the workshop participants, interviews were conducted with Chief Matapi through an interpreter (his grandson Kuripi) and in Portuguese with thirteen bilingual Wajãpi: ten researchers, one school teacher, and the presidents of the two existing organizations, the Wajãpi Council of Villages (APINA) and the Association of Wajãpi Indigenous Peoples of the Amapari Triangle (APIWATA).

At the time of my visit, nearly 20 indigenous researchers were staying at the *Kwapo'y wyry* village, next to the Aramirã Post, most of them men between 20 and 30 years old who came from various villages, accompanied by their immediate families.[4] In addition to them, the anthropologist mentioned, and the personnel from Iepé who provided logistical support to the activities and to the camp, employees of the National Indian Foundation (FUNAI) occasionally passed through in addition to others from the National Health Foundation (FUNASA), as well as other Wajãpi, heading to their villages or to Macapá. This indicates the high degree of contact that the group has with 'non-Indians', which is the category commonly used for outsiders.

Indeed, the Wajãpi have intense and varied contact with Brazilian state officials and national society, as well as with cultural and finance agencies and the international community of researchers. This circumstance makes it necessary for them to have a good knowledge of the Portuguese language and, at the same time, maintain and seek to strengthen their traditional language, which belongs to the Tupi group. However, Jawaruwa, who was one of the researchers attending the workshop, questioned the increasing use of Portuguese words when arguing about what he considers the most important domains of traditional culture:

---

[3] Information on the Wajãpi Program developed by Iepé is available at: http://www.institutoiepe. org.br/english/the-wajapi-programme.

[4] Interviews took place from 7 to 15 December 2008 with Aipi, Caubi, Japarupi, Jawapuku, Jawaruwa, Kupenã, Kuripi, Marãte, Matapi, Nazaré Ajãreaty, Parikura, and Rosenã.

J   More important? For example, our language…is more important to us
    because… For example, when we translate our language to another language
    of the karai kõ [non-Indians], of the whites … we have difficulty translating
    our language. So we use the language of the whites and are unable to make a
    correct translation

Besides the fact that, according to him, many Portuguese words do not have
corresponding terms in Wajãpi, difficulties in communication and intercultural
understanding are not limited to the sphere of language. Wajãpi people have been
the targets of prejudice and discrimination in Macapá, the capital city of Amapá
state. They report that they are harassed by passers-by who laugh, make catcalls,
and imitate Indian dances by tapping their hands to their mouths as seen in Hol-
lywood movies. They try to avoid the humiliating remarks by using clothes and
shoes (principally bras, pants and sneakers) or by adopting the styles and man-
nerisms of non-Indians (haircuts, make-up or cologne). As a way of repudiating
the stereotypes by which they are discriminated, some men prefer to not "dirty
their body" [draw *kusiwa* on their bodies] with *jenipapo* or *urucum*, principally
when they are not in the fields. Nazaré Ajãreaty (N) explained in an interview:

N   It's not just the boys, girls also want to use the clothes of the karai kõ; they
    want to be like the karai kõ. Men too, a young man who wants to be just like
    the karai kõ, uses shoes, cuts his hair, doesn't want to be an Indian, wants to
    be white, I don't know why.
A   Why?
N   We speak with the youth 'why do you change [cut] your hair? Do you want to
    date a karai kõ?' No, it seems… how do you call it? Indian bóio… I don't
    know. A prejudice, right.
A   Prejudice.
N   Wajãpi has no boió.
A   What is boió?
N   Bo…boiola.
A   Ah, boiola [gay].
N   That's it.
A   That's why a Wajãpi cuts his hair?
N   They say gay because he has long hair. That's it. For this reason when a youth
    goes to Macapá he cuts his hair. We say 'why do you cut your hair like that?'
    Because the whites say to us: 'you look like a woman with long hair. That's
    why we cut our hair'.

Not only is gender a source of humiliating stereotypes; they are also seen as
poor people, outsiders to the local economy. Rosenã, referring to how representations of rich and poor affect the values and attitudes of many young Wajãpi,
adds:

R   [Many youths] What they like most in the city is to see the things of the
     whites...they think everything is pretty...money as well. They think that
     money...they think that the whites earn money easily. In reality, only those who
     work earn money. Those who have a profession...only those people have money.
     They [many youths] think that we [if we] go live in the city, we would have
     money; [that] when we study in the city, we will have money. In reality, they
     only think of the things of whites... [they say with prejudice] 'this is poor, this
     one has nothing, has no money'. We, a few Wajãpi, know that we are not poor,
     we do not depend on the things [of] the non-Indian, we have the land, our land is
     rich. So, we do not depend on the non-Indian. We do the planting, we plant for
     our families, we have everything here on our land. We always say this to them.

In contrast with the praise—in Brazilian and international preservationist cir-
cles—of the *kusiwa* as a masterpiece of human or Brazilian cultural heritage, the
Wajãpi are not visible in the press and in local political and administrative fields.
There is little news in Amapá about their being the stakeholders of this patrimony,
and the official education programmes are slow to accept the need to include in the
curricula information about their culture, their right to difference, or other issues of
practical or political interest to them.

On the other hand, they have been developing, with the collaboration of academic partners and people from indigenous institutions, the training of indigenous
teachers and researchers. These educational activities developed by Iepé Institute,
that might well be identified as good practice in the field of ICH policy, have
contributed significantly to strengthening Wajãpi culture, and to creating two-way
access routes between traditional issues and concepts and subjects that arise from
the relations between this people and Brazilian and international society.

The training of agents capable of actively participating in this processes of
intercultural translation is an extremely important initiative; it helps the Indians
themselves to resolve the problems associated with their positioning in broader
social, economic and political structures. Wajãpi researchers (WR) and teachers
participate in the creation of a social space for interfacing and negotiation which is
essential for supporting the inter-ethnic relationships that they experience. This is one
of the spheres where Wajãpi political, cultural and socio-environmental agendas are
formed and developed. In recent years, intellectual property has become an important
issue on these agendas and the candidature of *kusiwa* to IPHAN and UNESCO has
been long matured within these activities before being officially submitted.

4.2 Origin, Possession and Transmission of *Kusiwa*

WR   In the past, there were no graphic paintings of the Wajãpi. With the passage
     of time, various paintings and colours arose. The collored paints came from
     the belly of the dead Cobra Grande [Big Snake]. The animals, birds and fish
     chose from it and took the colours to paint themselves.

At this time, the 'origin' [sic] of the Wajãpi participated and got the kusiwa paintings of the butterfly, pacu fish, surubim fish, macaws, monkeys etc. And the 'origin' of the Wajãpi participated and also got the paints from the belly of the dead Cobra Grande. At this time, the animals, birds and fish were like people and spoke a single language. Also at this time, the Wajãpi took advantage and learned the songs of birds and other animals and plants.

For this reason, we are not the owners of the kusiwa paintings, songs and festivals; but this immaterial knowledge remains for us, because we know and strengthen it until today.

Today there is also the jenipapo tree; it is very important, because this tree provides green fruits that we use to prepare the liquid [paint]. [We] take this liquid to [make] the various types of painting that we know.

Although this text is considered unfinished by the authors, it was prepared by a group of Indigenous researchers during a workshop that had the objective of clarifying for non-Indians the origin of the *kusiwa*. According to a personal statement by Gallois, since 2000 she has been regularly conducting activities in which old indigenous chiefs, researchers or teachers are encouraged by outside facilitators (anthropologists or others) to explain in their own language—and later to translate into Portuguese—what they judge important to say about their culture to the non-Indians. In this dialogical context they use written scripts, titles, illustrations. In other words, they appropriate formats that are commonly used by non-Indians in their own forms of expression.

Two important sources for my research resulted from this work conducted in workshops: the publications entitled *Ia ma'e kõ*, about 'the owners', which was concluded in 2006, and *I'a*, about 'doubles' and images, completed in 2008. Besides this, in response to issues raised by me in their workshops, they produced written texts and recorded interviews. I will briefly review some of these documents.

The narrative about the genesis of the *kusiwa* refers to time immemorial, to times of undifferentiation, '*when all spoke the same language*', as well as to the action of the '*animals, birds and fish*' who '*chose and took*' from the belly of the Cobra Grande the paints to paint themselves and, finally, to the agency of the '*origin of the Wajãpi*', which I interpret as the 'Wajãpi ancestors', who became possessors of *kusiwa* and left it as a legacy to this people. The ancestors had 'learned' *kusiwa*, songs and festivals, as would be seen later, from '*the owners*'. The text reproduced above and read to me by Jawapuku affirms '*we are not owners of the kusiwa; but this knowledge remains for us*' [*permanece para nós*] because the Wajãpi have practised it and strengthened it over time. That is, the possession of this form of cultural expression appears to be made legitimate by an ancestral legacy, as well as by the creative and continued practice of many generations of descendants.

To be the '*owner*' of something is not an expression that should be understood here at face value and interpreted according to the meaning usually attributed to it in other cultural contexts. It is a linguistic construction that would describe, in

Portuguese, the relationship between the *I'jã* and things. The youth Kupenã (K) explains with greater detail to the anthropologist (A) the Wajãpi use of the Portuguese word *'dono'* [owner], navigating in intercultural waters:

K   There is [an] owner of the trees, there is [an] owner of the rivers, there is [an] owner of the earth, [there is an] owner of the stones, there is [an] owner of the mountain, and there is [an] owner of the marshy forest, there is [an] owner... how do you call it? Of dense forests... that's how it is.

A   Do people have an owner?

K   Yes.

A   Who is it?

K   We call him Janaijã... Jesus.

A   The creator?

K   Our creator. [For] this reason we call him the 'owner' because he created [us], do you understand?

A   I understand. Not that he is the owner in the sense that he can give or sell someone or something. He is the owner because he created the person (...), because he created that animal.

K   Like we raise animals; [the animal] has an owner because he [the owner] created it. So there is an owner.

A   What is the word for owner in Wajãpi?

K   I'jã.

According to Kupenã, the owner is the one who conceives, gives life, raises, protects, cares, cultivates; the creator remains—as will be seen below—linked to the creation, even when others are allowed access to them, as happened with the Wajãpi ancestors. The chief Matapi, who is a respected man among the elders, expands on the explanation by highlighting, in the notion of 'owner', the concept of 'guardian', and in terms of possession, the idea of commitment and punishment for one who exercises some form of appropriation not authorized by custom. He (M) explained, with his grandson Kuripi (K) to interpret:

M/K   He said that the butterfly has an owner (...) that a butterfly that always flies by here does not live without an owner (...) in reality the owner sees the butterflies, he sees when someone kills the butterfly and he makes something happen to this person, because he killed the butterfly and so the owner gets angry. Then he gives the person a fever or... he could get sick, or something happens. The person begins to tremble too, and it will always be like this.

A   And if a kusiwa is made of the butterfly?

M/K   He said that when we paint with jenipapo, when we design the butterfly, the owner also becomes happy, nothing happens to the person, because he sees that the person is painting and is pleased; (...) because this design of the butterfly is truly traditional. It's not for any person [to make] (...) it's just for us, because this knowledge came just for us, it's not for any person. For example [the] non-indigenous wants to see and study this knowledge, we will not authorize this (...) because [if we did so], we would not be at ease...we would be quite concerned (...) we learned this knowledge from the butterfly owner, [it was] he who gave this knowledge to us and we discovered and practised it.

The authorized practice of the *kusiwa* is that made 'with knowledge' in at least three senses: (1) technical knowledge, which is transmitted between members of the same families in the local groups; (2) with understanding of the meanings expressed by the motifs designed and which belong to Wajãpi cosmology; and (3) with observance of the prohibitions established, since time immemorial, by the 'owners' (*I'jã*) for the Wajãpi ancestors. These interdictions recognize and reinforce the belief in the mystical power of the *kusiwa* and for this reason, they are observed by the current heirs, who are the legitimate practitioners of the *kusiwa*. They use the graphics both to decorate and to protect their bodies.

The text read by Kupenã (Wajãpi Researchers 2008), which was produced by another group of researchers, shows that learning the *kusiwa* implies becoming capable of reproducing the graphic motifs and combining them, creating new compositions, as occurs, by the way, in other forms of language:

WR   We Wajãpi have different customs of making the design of the painting, for example, designs of the butterfly combined with fish scales. We do not always copy how another person painted them; we think and invent a way of combining the *kusiwa* standards to make the composition (...) the person learns many types of designs and combines them differently.

     The young people do not learn alone to make painting. They learn with their father, their mother and with other people (...) Painting is not easy to learn quickly; [it is] like (...) learning to write for the first time with a pencil.

Reading another text produced by the indigenous researchers about what they interpreted as 'rules for Wajãpi graphic arts', Rosenã discussed the nature of the connection between the 'owner' and those who were authorized to 'imitate' the ancestral paintings on their bodies, or that is, draw them. It is worth noting that the action of designing (imitating) is understood here as a way of performing pre-existing motifs, whose symbolic power is controlled by the 'owners' of things, the *I'jã*. The narrative of Rosenã clarifies the use of spells and interdictions:

R   Only the people who are not under ritual interdiction can imitate paintings on their bodies. From the origin, our ancestors knew these rules which we continue to use and respect today. In the past, [when] the animals spoke like humans, each owner of the paintings explained his rules of the paintings to our ancestors [who] learned them. The owners of the paintings spoke to our ancestors: you cannot imitate my paintings on newborns and [on] who has a newborn and [on] a young woman who is menstruating.

They also told our ancestors: we will always keep a watch on our paintings. If you use them or do not respect these rules, we will get angry and cast a spell on this person who used our painting improperly. The owners of the things do not appear; only the invisible appears [which is seen only through the shaman's mirror]. For this reason we continue to do this until today.

Although these interdictions are frequently mentioned, it appears that there is no impediment to the 'imitation' by the Wajãpi of the graphic, choreographic or musical motifs of other peoples. On the contrary, this seems to be a widely accepted source of inspiration for their cultural enrichment. The brochure *I'ã* states: "for us the Wajãpi, a'ãga is imitation. For example, (…) when we visit another village and see some artefacts, later we return (…) and we imitate that artefact that we saw. (…) We also imitate the roar of the jaguar and bird songs (…) a canoe made by another group and their houses (…) somebody paintings" (Professores Wajãpi 2008, p. 23). It can be presumed, therefore, that motifs and objects of other peoples and cultures are considered to be, in a manner of speaking, of free access. Because they are not transmitted, used and reproduced in the space regulated by the Wajãpi custom, they can be freely practised, and they probably also acquire new meanings in the contexts to which they are transferred.

Nevertheless, Rosenã warns of another important aspect of the issue: '*to imitate*' also means recognizing as belonging to others. The link of origin is not automatically erased in the copy; its omission can at least reveal that it is a counterfeit:

R   These days we travel a lot (….) [to] visit [other] indigenous peoples, to exchange experiences. At times we imitate graphic art that other peoples use, we imitate it. But we know that is the art of other peoples and we know [it is not] our art.

A   You don't mix one with the other.

R   We don't mix them. Here in our village that painting does not exist, we know that it is from another people. When other people tell a story, we also bring them here to tell it in our area… [our] village; what other people think about the relation to forests… And [in the case of] festivals, it's difficult, isn't it? A festival is different. They sing differently as well, [the] other peoples. We don't even know their language, [so] it is difficult to copy festivals.

A   Because the language is different.

R   The language is different. Others… others are craftspersons whom we imitate, we learn with them. We learn and we bring here to imitate for the community to see.

A   Do you think that this is interesting? That there is an exchange between cultures (…) Do you think this is something good or something bad?

R   Learning from the other?

M   Yes.

R   It depends on the people, right? Some people went there and weren't interested in this, and did not learn as well. But it's good isn't it? When going to the other… visiting other indigenous peoples, we have to show our culture to that people. This is our knowledge, this is how we live, this is our *kusiwa*, because each *kusiwa* has a meaning behind it. This has to be shown as well for the indigenous peoples to know…because they have to know… later, when some people take this body painting to them and say 'this is mine', when someone sees it, they will say 'this is Wajãpi'. They will warn them.

It is relevant, in order to adequately understand this aspect of the problem, to note that Japarupi (J) identifies a certain degree of naivety in the use of *kusiwa* motifs by outsiders when he comments on the designs that Marãte made on my arm, as had also occurred with other visitors:

J   The painting that you are using here [indicating my arm] you know nothing about the history. Inside here there is a history; each painting that we use has a history different from the other design.
C   For me, this here is a memory that I am taking of this week that I spent here…So, when I look at my arm, I remember that I was here, that I liked it, that it was good.
J   Well, inside here there is much history, that to write…

In the *kusiwa*, as in other practices and knowledge codified by custom, the interviewees make clear that access is inherent to the positions that the subjects occupy in society. Japarupi (J) explains:

J   I, for example, I know how to do that, but women do not know; and [there are] women who know, and I don't know. And there are 60–70 year old adults who know how to do things that I don't know. (…) For example, my father can teach me, but somebody else's father, my oldest relative, can't. Or he [the relative] can speak with my father, or my father can teach him, and he [my father] can pass it on to me. (…) Then, things that I learned with him, I will pass to you? No! It's not like that. It is slow, when one reaches 70…then it can be told.
A   When you speak to a researcher and you tell what you learned (…) the researcher publishes and any person finds out.
J   These days, for us [to] show to a non-Indian…to respect… then, we show [in] writing in a notebook (…) Another thing, that shouldn't be told, we wouldn't talk about it. (…) I can tell my son, but my son who is twenty or thirty, I can tell it like that.
C   When he is old enough to know?
J   That's right, I can't tell a twelve-year-old child because he will tell. Because a child, when we tell something to him, he tells everyone.

4.3 *Jane'ã* and *a'ãga*: Vital Principle, Image and the Double

The Wajãpi understand that something of the person or of the object made or represented—which they translate as "its vital principle"—is present in the artefacts, in the imitations and in the designs in particular. "During life, a person works a lot and constructs things: a house, crafts, arrows, etc. For this reason, the marks of the hands (*ipoãgwerã*) and the soul (*i'ã*) of a person stay forever on these artefacts" (Professores Wajãpi 2008, p. 3).

The issue is even more sensitive when referring to photographic or audiovisual images ('imitations'). "The photo and the image in the film are like a double of the person. But there is *i'ã* behind the photos, which is invisible. (…) When we take an image *ta'ãga* of the person to send to some place, *i'ã* goes with it and also *opiwarã*. (…) When we record a person's speech, *i'ã* and *opiwarã* go with the recording" (Professores Wajãpi 2008, pp. 26–27).

Japarupi's comments about photography are extremely valuable for understanding the sense of the rules established by the Wajãpi about capturing images, mainly the restrictions made on the audio and visual recordings produced by non-Indians, as well as their motivation for learning to use audiovisual technology.

A   Yes. There are many stories that I don't know. And with photography, in the case of the people who take pictures of the Wajãpi?

J   That's it, as I said, there are secrets…secrets. I don't know if I can tell you, but… I have to ask the chief for authorization to tell. But… (…) for us, the Wajãpi cannot take a picture of his relative. So I can't, I can't take his picture because [he would ask:] 'what will you do with my photo? Where will you take it?' I can't. I can take a picture with him; but alone, I can't take a picture. (…) This photo there on the poster [indicates a poster on the wall portraying a female Indian] no one touches, no one will do anything with it, she is there, I know that she will stay here protected; a non-Indian will not take it to throw it here or there and do who knows what with it. Non-Indians…to take a picture…One has to take it to keep it, so that in the future the son can see the photo of his father.

A   Can you take a picture of your sons?

J   I can.

A   Can your sons take a picture of you?

J   They can.

A   Can you take pictures of your brothers?

J   I think I can't, no…together with him I can, separately I can't. For example, I know that my brother is not… my brother, for example, I cannot take a picture of my brother's wife. My brother does not trust me. Because many people enter my house, they could take it, they will see [the picture]. So I cannot take a picture of her.

A   And of a relative from another village?

J   In the past we got married to someone betrothed. Today it's not like that, we marry in another village, here and there (…) if I marry [with] a woman from another village (…) perhaps she will get angry, take that photo of my brother, of my nephew and do something wrong with it, then [I am] the guilty person, because my brother will say: 'That photo that you took [of me], do you have it? No! I look for it and don't find it'. (…)

A   So, you can only take a picture when there is trust?

J   Yes, trust. (…) These days, the elders [are] saying that non-Indians cannot take photos because non-Indians take the soul very far, our spirit, and we wind up becoming weak…they don't let non-Indians [to] take photos any more. There [is] a woman [indicates the poster with the photo of the female Indian]. She is a woman. But the spirit, her soul, is suffering there, it never returned to her village. Then one shouldn't let them [to photograph]…it is complicated for us, photos can't be taken. Because she [the woman in the poster] is there, the owner is travelling there… (…) and the photo here is suffering, no one knows… (…)

A   It turns yellow…

J   We are also beginning to think of not letting them film anymore, because the person winds up travelling there inside… it's sad…not being there, the spirit… because we wind up not seeing… not bringing [something] good for us, no… when one sees television, travels there inside the television, it doesn't work…when non-Indians enter the [indigenous] area, they can't, they really can't film, because it is very bad for their spirit, they don't want to send it out.

The initiative of applying for the listing of *kusiwa* graphics by the Institute of National Historical and Artistic Heritage (IPHAN) as well as the proposal for the proclamation as a Masterpiece of Oral and Intangible Heritage of Humanity by UNESCO were motivated by the Wajãpi's protests about the improper use of their image. The Amapá government had used the photograph of an Indian woman who had committed suicide in a promotional shirt, as well as images of Indians in billboards, which triggered a movement to raise awareness and protest against the improper use of images.

For these reasons, Rosenã explained in an interview, it is necessary to warn non-Indians about the dangers of photographing a Wajãpi, especially a shaman, to whom is attributed the power of making spells:

R   Mainly a shaman, the photo of a shaman… When it travels to another country, for other peoples to see, then they will soon see, [the] other Indians, that this [man photographed] is a shaman, because they will also see his spirit, his substance. He is a shaman! They will see. Then, later, he will seek revenge, that shaman, in our village. For this reason, it [is] dangerous to take a picture of a shaman, according to our knowledge.

A   Why?

R   (…). He orders people to die. That's why.

4.4 Intellectual Rights Regulation: Between the Custom and the Laws

During my fieldwork, as was expected, difficulties arose over the notions covered by the semantic fields of intellectual property and intellectual rights. Following the usual strategy of the workshops, the basic elements of these concepts and their most immediate implications were presented; and complementary to this, it was proposed that they reformulate these in their own terms, according to their own understanding of the matter, so that they could be adequately understood by the elders. The intention of this complex exercise was that they should work simultaneously with Western juridical principles and with local knowledge. With the participation of Gallois and myself, they reached the synthetic phrase '*I jarã omarã kuwa rupi te oinõ momae'ko*', which can be interpreted as: 'the owner is one that makes things with knowledge, in the route of experience'.

From the standpoint of the discussions that took place during the workshop this statement seems to condense the following basic ideas: (1) the moral foundation of ownership depends on the person in question belonging to the social group, and thus having legitimate access to the sources of knowledge; (2) there is an intrinsic relationship between ownership and socially accepted practice; (3) the legitimate basis of practice means commitment to the symbolic meanings of the know-how; and (4) tradition can creatively meet with innovation through the experience of living in a changing context.

They are quite aware of the fact that in order to be included in public policies, a balance must be achieved between custom and formal law and that this achievement depends on the efforts made by both government officials and the Wajãpi.

Brazilian legislation establishes that requests for authorization of access to indigenous lands for research purposes must be submitted to the Indians themselves, to the National Indian Foundation (FUNAI), to the Scientific and Technological Development Council (CNPq) and, when it concerns traditional knowledge associated to genetic heritage, to the Genetic Heritage Management Council (CGEN). This legislation has been applied with substantial rigour. Concerning the Wajãpi, it is important to mention the efforts made by their researchers, assisted by Iepé partners, to expand the knowledge of the Indians themselves and of the outside public about the legal and moral problems related to the production of audiovisual records and collection of ethnographic materials.

The publication *I'ã*, mentioned a few times in preceding pages, concludes with the affirmation that, in relation to production and dissemination of images, 'we researchers will advise non-Indians so problems do not occur'. I consulted some people about what these warnings might be and discussed this statement with them, collectively, in a workshop session. Their opinions about the possible retaliations oscillated between the traditional forms of control—whether by spells or blows from a stick (mentioned jokingly)—and the experience accumulated through the application of legal norms.

The following formulation of requests for authorization to conduct research and produce audio and/or visual documentation among the Wajãpi was reached in the workshop, but had not been finalized by the end of my visit. According to the participants (this is not an official decision of APINA or APIWATA) it would be necessary to meet the following requirements:

1. *Identify the proponent in detail, declare his or her place of residence and most efficient forms of contact (telephone, email, etc.).* [One of the objectives of this request is to respond to the need to fast localization of the solicitant in case of conflict or transgression of any agreement].

2. *Request authorization to conduct the work, initially sending the documentation to APINA and APIWATA, who will make a preliminary response and send it to FUNAI, CNPq, and also CGEN, when necessary. The approval of the request by the indigenous organizations will be discussed after the other agencies issue a position.* [This procedure would invert the usual process which, today, is initiated at the official agencies, suggesting the Wajãpi's desire to establish direct communication with any proponents; the Wajãpi would reserve the right to the last word about the issue after hearing the official agencies and consulting all and every one of the chiefs of the various villages, either by radio or in assembly if necessary].

3. *Present in detail the objectives of the project or the proposal, specifying if the activities will have commercial purposes or not, and the forms of dissemination of the results.* [This involves the need to send a previous and informed authorization request, suitably clear and detailed].

4. *If the request is approved, the terms of agreement must be signed, indicating material and moral elements of the transaction and establishing penalties for non-compliance.* [The difficulty of enforcing a term of agreement was raised, in relation to which the action of government authorities, allies and partners were mentioned as possible methods].

5. *Deposit integral copies of the results of the work undertaken and of the registrations realized at the Wajãpi Documentation Centre, in Aramirã.* [This documentation centre is being built in Aramirã with resources provided by private sponsors and as part of the *Kusiwa* Safeguarding Action Plan. Suitable equipment is being purchased and personnel trained to receive, conserve and make this collection available for consultation].

6. *Register the term of agreement with a notary public.* [The use of a public document seeks to reinforce the effectiveness of the measures of the sanction].

In the consultations and debates I observed that the implementation of a collective decision-making process does not appear to be a particularly significant problem among them. All of the villages are interlinked by a radio system that not only allows communication between them but also with the main offices of the APINA and APIWATA, in Macapá. The mechanism currently used was described in the following terms: requests for authorization, as well as other documents, are sent to the APINA offices in Macapá; from there they are sent to APIWATA and to the chiefs of the various villages who, after discussing the issue in their localities and between themselves, contact the entity. If there are differing positions, they try to reach a decision that is acceptable to all. Therefore, the tendency is not to decide by majority but by consensus. In the cases in which the authorization involves material benefits, these are sent to APINA, which uses them in support of everyone, or redistributes them following ad hoc deliberation.

Considering the limited character of this fieldwork, it was not possible to determine to what degree this system effectively functions and how the conflicts that certainly occur are resolved. Even if there are tensions and eventual problems, various statements corroborate the conclusion that, in principle, this process appears to make viable internal consultations and external communication of the Wajãpi in various types of negotiations.

In relation to the use of formal legal instruments concerning copyright and the rights of the interpreter by the Wajãpi, until now there has been only one case, which was the registration of the book entitled *I'ã ma'e kõ* at the Brazilian National Library. For this work, which had financial support from the Ministry of Education, the generic denomination 'Professores Wajãpi' [Wajãpi Teachers] was used to indicate authorship and the book included lists of the names of the authors of the texts or of the drawings, the usual credits of those responsible for specific aspects of a publication, and an explanatory note about how the work was conducted.

4.5 Closing Remarks

A few comments should be made before concluding this brief account of the practices developed by the Wajãpi with a view to regulating the transmission, transformation, documentation, dissemination and safeguarding of aspects of their own culture as heritage.

It is common knowledge in anthropology that (1) there are always contrasting and, at times, conflicting versions of narratives, and that in such cases no version is truer than another; (2) this being so, the most relevant ethnographic evidence is variability within a given social context; (3) this variability suggests that there is a twilight zone of beliefs and values where disagreements are made explicit and disputes can be settled in ways prescribed by local custom.

The relevance of bringing in these issues at this point of my argument is that it must be clear to the reader that the present notes are not intended to be either a complete version of the facts concerning the regulations and practices of the Wajãpi, nor the expression of a supposedly community consensus on the subject. It is a fact that many passages of my text refer to views that were publicly discussed and agreed upon by the indigenous researchers who happened to be in the village at the time of my visit. It is also true that the supporting evidence of my argument has been cross-checked with various individuals and with the Iepé anthropologists who have been studying this culture for several years.

My modest intention here is to delineate the themes that give a particular shape to this zone of uncertainty, and to highlight the topics that seemed to me, in this very brief encounter, to be a part of the problem of safeguarding intangible cultural heritage from the Wajãpi's point of view. More comparative work must be carried out before making any generalizations. However, it seems that the greater difficulties in this field, particularly in relation to customary and legal conceptions about intellectual rights—in the Wajãpi case at least—lie not in the mechanics or the politics of obtaining previous informed consent, as often has been suggested, but in taking seriously and respecting the deeper cultural issues embedded in what is called, in Western juridical jargon, rights to the image, rights of interpretation of one's cultural traditions and of political self-determination.

References

Arantes, A. A, 2009: Documenting and disseminating traditional knowledge and cultural expressions in Brazil. Vol. 1: Survey (147 p.) Legislation, institutional guidelines and instruments. (406. p.): (Geneva: WIPO. Available at http://www.wipo.int/tk/en/culturalheritage/surveys.html
Gallois, Dominique T, 2002: "Expressão Gráfica e Oralidade entre os Wajãpi do Amapá." Boletim do Museu do Índio. Documentação, n° 9, Rio de Janeiro: Museu do Índio.
Professores W, 2008: I'ã Macapá: Iepé/Apina.
Wajãpi R, 2008: The origin of the *kusiwa* (In preparation).

Chapter 5
Challenges for Anthropological Research on Intangible Cultural Heritage

Jesús Antonio Machuca

5.1 Differences Between Culture and Cultural Heritage

The notion of culture is the central and most representative category in anthropology, whereas the notion of cultural heritage comes from a different source. It has two principal branches: on the one hand, succession to property and financial wealth, which occurs through the paternal line; and on the other, the reference to certain goods that are representative and of a symbolic nature that a community has processed selectively and with which it identifies itself.

It could be said up that up to a certain point, the category of cultural heritage originated outside the field in which anthropology has constructed its study object. Rather, this notion is related to the historical-social production of the principal symbolic references of a people-nation, and this plays a political and ideological role in modern societies. From that perspective, heritage is also an idea that refers to the affective and ideological-identity aspect of the inhabitants in their social formation and is expressed or crystallized in certain elements playing a referential role (emblems, memory sites, etc.) and corresponding to an identity and a recognition.

There is a close parallel between the symbolic representation of heritage as a good that is withdrawn from circulation and separated from other cultural goods as a significant or representative entity and the process through which those in power withdraw certain goods from circulation in order to accumulate them as wealth, serving as support for power. Heritage serves, in turn, as a symbolic equivalent of material wealth. Culture, economy and power are thus closely associated in a relationship of mutual remission.

J. A. Machuca (✉)
DEAS-INAH, Av. San Jerónimo núm. 880, Col. San Jerónimo Lídice, Delegación Magdalena Contreras C.P. 10200, Mexico, D.F., Mexico
e-mail: machucaantonio@hotmail.com

L. Arizpe and C. Amescua (eds.), *Anthropological Perspectives on Intangible Cultural Heritage*, SpringerBriefs in Environment, Security, Development and Peace 6, DOI: 10.1007/978-3-319-00855-4_5, © The Author(s) 2013

The aspects to which the problems of heritage are related are so varied that a number of disciplines, such as semiotics, history, historical architecture, sociology, legal science, and anthropology are joined in them.

5.2 The Symbolic-Intangible Permeability of Culture

Intangible cultural heritage is, in addition, the terrain of social and symbolic representations (including knowledge, beliefs and forms of social imaginary) such as myths, narratives and beliefs, but also of acquired behavioural forms, such as skills or outlines of practical arrangements. That is to say, it is in turn broken down into two aspects: representational and practical, and also into two intentionalities that denote ways of acting and relating to the world: the symbolic way and the practical-utilitarian way, respectively, which are linked to each other.[1]

For example, studies made from the intangible perspective of culture (semiotic or symbolic) with reference to historical information can discern principles and stylistic codes or mindsets and can demonstrate how the ideological and symbolic aspect permeates and underlies the organization of realizations of a material order, such as the social logic underlying the arrangement of spaces. In the twentieth century, the emblematic monuments of nationalism stood out in this aspect. In this sense, there does not appear to be any cognitive obstacle whatsoever in the material culture to visualization of the intangible part.

In reality, there is no material cultural heritage that separates itself in a relevant way from another that is characterized epistemologically as intangible. Culture (material or intangible) is by definition symbolic.[2] We can see that certain kinds of knowledge that are applied—such as activities and skills—in the production of a specific good incorporate a symbolic value into that good. In addition, these same objects play an analogous role in a determined semantic field in which they accompany certain practices, so that they acquire a symbolic effectiveness.

It would appear that the opposition between material and intangible culture is most obviously seen in the difference between the phenomenal and living manifestation of culture on the one hand and its objective monumental products on the other. However, this difference does not count in the analysis of meanings, which covers both.

The anthropological analysis that takes cultural heritage as a knowledge object and material for study is thus faced with the task of discerning meanings expressed in very diverse and expressive supports and practices: general representations of the cosmos and nature; performative forms such as rituals, dances and musicals in their fullest extent; gestural and linguistic or corporally represented expressions.

---

[1] Remember Habermas' approach in this regard, as, for example, in *Technik und Wissenschaft als 'Ideologie'* (1968) (English translation: *Technology and Science as 'Ideology'*).

[2] This can be seen, for example, in Appadurai's definition (2001).

Cultural heritage is a good that is not accumulated but above all is transmitted between persons and generations.

A critical-semiotic analysis of the monumentalist conception of culture also shows it to be an eminently ideological construction. Hence, by unveiling epistemologically and conceptually what has been conceived from that perspective as cultural heritage, it can be seen that a form of conception has been produced based on a *synecdoche* by which cultural heritage is reduced to its monumental expressions (the part for the whole).

5.3 The End of the Paradigm of the Cultural Heritage of the State and the Emergence of Another

Cultural heritage is a product decanted from the living process of culture and has specific historical and social modalities. The concept is associated with that of the historical formation of the modern state and its appropriation processes and notions of public and social property. In countries like Mexico, it reached its culmination in nationalism. Its initial frame of reference was the legal-political and ideological form of the nation's property, adopted and developed principally from the nineteenth century to the mid-twentieth century.

The prevailing interest in and approach to cultural heritage in countries like Mexico come from the institutions themselves. It has also been visualized as the social process of constructing identity references in national society.[3] From that perspective, a concept of cultural heritage has been coined closely associated with the formation of the nation state, although—as we know—the formation of this heritage extends beyond those conditions. The modern concept of it as a collective good and identity reference is produced from a relationship in which the state is reflected in it, an extension of its hegemony. In that sense, some of the fetishism found in the state is also reproduced in that heritage.

The cohesive function of this notion is therefore clear; there is also a posthumous consensus in which up to a certain point differences are reconciled, presupposing a long and painful trail of political and symbolic disputes among social groups throughout a process that has led to the elevation of a hegemonic social sector.

Questions can be asked about the changes that may have occurred as a consequence of globalization and the cultural shift produced in the course of the century, changes which have signified the loss of the validity of the nation-state paradigm of heritage.

In such a case, full achievement of the objectives of conventions such as that on *Cultural Diversity* and the *Convention for the Safeguarding of Intangible Cultural*

---

[3] This is the case of the book coordinated by Florescano (1993), *El Patrimonio Cultural de México,* or that of Françoise Choay (1992), *L'Allégorie du Patrimoine.*

Fig. 5.1 Research planning meeting on intangible cultural heritage, CRIM–UNAM, Cuernavaca, Morelos (2012). *Source* Photo by Carolina Buenrostro

Heritage would require an adequate legal-political framework and a state that was not only formally pluricultural but genuinely participative and that would guarantee cultural democracy, as well as one in which effective restrictions could be placed on the more avaricious interests of transnational companies that exploit the resources of ethno-cultural regions (Fig. 5.1).

5.4 Movement Towards an Anthropological Concept of Heritage

The notion of intangible cultural heritage on which our attention is currently focused comes via another route. Its origin is related to the development of anthropology and the study of and contact with numerous societies characterized by social relations based on forms of exchange and cooperation involving reciprocity, as well as a close, more direct relationship with utilization of the environment.

Intangible heritage becomes important where a large part of production results from the application of manual and artisanal skills, including forms of knowledge, beliefs and lifestyles, as well as practical-symbolic systems linked to a variety of representations. A characteristic of intangible cultural heritage is its singularity.

Cultural diversity is also conceived as being the culture of singularities and is less linked with any presumption of universality. In this area, interculturalism refers in turn to something very different from cultural hegemony (which was expressed in the motto: one nation, one culture) that prevailed as the best means of achieving supremacy and political hegemony from the second half of the nineteenth century until the middle of the twentieth century. Thus, in the framework of post-revolutionary governments, alliance with cultural movements became something like astuteness in nation-state projects, since by then culture was achieving consensuses that were not being attained in the direct terrain of politics.

The approximation between the notion of cultural heritage and culture itself has had the advantage of permitting a breakaway from the scleroticized concept of heritage. On the other hand, it is necessary not to lose sight of the difference between culture and heritage. Heritage implies identity; a feeling of social (and affective) appropriation; the production of a historical meaning for a social group; the concept of an inherited good that in turn must be passed on, which converts it into a connection (and a reference that serves to reinforce the relationship) between the past and the future. In short, it represents a lasting form of consolidation and crystallization of what is dynamic and fluid in the culture. In addition to being a reference (charged with representing a diversity of meanings, in a more or less substantial way), it has the characteristic of hiding the process that has led it to that function and elevation.

5.5 Consequences of a New Paradigm of Intangible Cultural Heritage

In the last decade, we have observed the phenomenon of an extension of the notion of heritage into the cultural sphere, as well as, and principally, a cognitive movement from a form of *episteme* (or way of knowing) centred on objects towards one with an emphasis on living processes and manifestations; this has had unprecedented consequences, whose effects have been felt in recent years.

Indeed, demands have arisen from a number of peoples for recognition and recovery of what they consider to be their own culture, whereas for governments and other economic forces, the resource of heritage plays a role as a factor in negotiation, as in the case of identities. However, negotiation becomes something problematical from which both a reaffirmation and a resignification of cultural references might be produced, as well as the possibility of a cultural loss accepted voluntarily by the bearers of the culture themselves.

Likewise, the positioning that many assume to represent recognition of their heritage with the expectation of its being included in the UNESCO Lists and Proclamations has encouraged and led to the existence of a multiplicity of social players who strive for promotion of the cultural good associated with its economic value.

   The phenomenon of generalized cultural patrimonialization that has been fostered in this way leads to the formulation of the hypothesis that an acceleration effect is occurring with respect to the time taken for the production and selection (reduced to a minimum) of the goods. The most outstanding exponents of the culture are usually required in order for it to acquire value and significance as cultural heritage.

   Intangible culture, in general, tends in turn to be considered as heritage, and this leads to confusion between culture and heritage. This could be a symptom of renewed zeal in the search for identity factors, as well as an attitude of appropriating something that can provide a renewed meaning. But it can also indicate that cultural patrimonialization is an emblem of prestige, as well as, more importantly, an economic advantage in a society with a bent towards tourism.

   On the other hand, if that heritage is faced by the threat of being despoiled, a reactive phenomenon is generated in defence. This supports the conclusion that its depositaries and bearers also manifest themselves as subjects (individual and collective) who tend to assume control, orientation and use of the heritage. And so here there is a research scenario: the relation of social movements to cultural heritage, and how they take it and give it a new significance.

   Anthropological research has also taken a new turn in the sense that what it processes and generates has to pass through the viewpoint and meanings that the social players themselves give it as subjects of the cultures studied. This makes it obvious that there is a need to recognize the cognitive autonomy of the subject peoples. With this, hermeneutics has abandoned the privileged perspective of the interpreter with a viewpoint that presumes to show the truth. For that reason, this approach, associated with romantic prosody, has been taken more seriously and acquired renewed importance with an impetus from postmodern anthropology. Now it is necessary rather to confront and evaluate various cognitive perspectives and establish an intersubjective relationship that applies recurrent and intercultural adjustments. The dilemma of the *emic* approach (the native's cultural perspective) and the *etic* approach (the anthropologist's scientific perspective) is followed by a tilting towards the interaction of dialogicity (following the line taken by Bajtín and Habermas).

5.6 The Other Side of the Invisibilization of Culture

There is an aspect of culture that has been overlooked in the *Convention for the Safeguarding of Cultural Heritage* but which anthropology nevertheless studies with great interest. It is the aspect of culture that involves its own destruction or that affects the lives of human beings to some degree. It can be identified in certain precepts, rules and actions, as well as in rites of passage, propitiatory sacrifices, etc.

   A related question is whether certain practices that are unacceptable to Western culture can become part of the cultural heritage, since they are accepted by existing cultural and religious systems. What we want to propose is that if they are rejected because they violate human rights, they nevertheless do not cease to be subject matter for research just because of that. In a similar way, aspects and forms of behaviour are being discovered in the Western world that denote logics that are concealed or disguised by the culture itself, and which resemble those outside the Western world that are widely rejected.

It is now considered that these phenomena represent the hidden face of culture and that if this is not taken into account, much of what is identified in the visible part of the culture would not be sufficiently known and would even be incomprehensible. Discerning these phenomena can clarify aspects whose logic has not yet been fully elucidated.

We have come to consider that culture is not only the politically correct part recorded and proclaimed in the Conventions. The constructive part of culture, according to this, would have as a counterpart a component involving wastefulness and an aspect of destruction also found in nature. This can be seen, for example, in the various forms of symbolic destruction of cultural goods performed at certain intervals in various regions of the world, such as those accompanying and representing *potlatch*, studied by many anthropologists such as Ruth Benedict.

It should be considered that culture is not a homogeneous whole. In addition, certain aspects of it may appear to be the culmination of destructive processes, or rather to be in themselves resembling an aspect of manifestations of 'barbarism'. Ritual manifestations that are eminently cultural are sometimes also bloody, sacrificial occurrences. In the name of certain traditions, there are not infrequently practices in certain cultures that affect life or gender condition. These are generally forms where integrist cultural structures or ideologies of a patriarchal type prevail at base. Anthropological research encounters problems that involve the scholar ethically and politically.

5.7 Importance of Research in Offering Alternatives to the Challenges of Development

In present-day society, access to intangible goods and services is growing. In addition, knowledge holds an ever larger place in social and value production. Conceptual systems play a decisive role in the orientation and management of very different productive processes.

In turn, the approval of the *Convention for the Safeguarding of Intangible Heritage* has coincided with a transition towards an era of the exploitation of intangible goods (cultural, aesthetic, symbolic and cognitive). The trends in cognitive capitalism are advancing not only by capturing information about the properties of plants and their active principles, but also about vernacular interpretive systems or the designs for artisanal production that refer to knowledge that is "reproducible in unlimited quantities at almost no cost" (Gorz 2003a, b).[4]

There is no doubt that intangible heritage is involved in this trend. Anthropological research in this sense is not faced by intact niches of preservation of millenary knowledge and representations, but rather by goods that could be widely plundered for the benefit of third parties. This panorama would make it obligatory to adopt a certain disposition of research strategies. It could be fruitful if it proceeds in a democratic and social way, and if researchers are aware that it will be necessary to contribute to safeguarding the goods not only in their vernacular contexts but also in the new scenario of a knowledge and market society to which the depositaries and bearers of the heritage have already acceded.

The uniqueness of each culture is distinguished by the way in which each group relates historically to its setting. For this reason, it has been possible to observe the adaptability and plasticity of communities possessing traditional knowledge when faced by the impact of climate change, inasmuch as not very long ago a crisis was being diagnosed in interpretive systems based on stable cycles in nature.

Climate change can cause certain practices to no longer have an effect and even to be the cause of a breakdown of the cultural capacity to carry out diagnoses in the field of the phenological markers[5] that serve to calculate the probability of rain or drought based on the appearance of plants or insects and bird migrations.

However, as indicated in a study by Briones (2011), it has also been observed that the communities are developing adaptive mechanisms: adjustment rituals, when faced by climate uncertainty, that advance or delay planting. This results in changes in economic and symbolic-ritual behaviour.

The different ways of managing ecosystems based on ethnic and traditional knowledge and cultural technologies can play a very important role in the transition to an alternative rationality and a new, sustainable relationship with the environment. For example, anthropological perspectivism recognizes concepts of identity and subjectivity that underlie behaviours integrated in a different way into the environment. And a sense of non-plundering of resources is recovered in the concept of good living promoted among the indigenous peoples of South America, as well as the idea that the concept of Mother Earth subsumes the conviction that affecting part of a living system may have consequences for others, so that rights in this sphere necessarily involve its preservation.

This field of relationship: between a certain cosmic vision, a system of ethically and culturally regulated utilization and the rights derived from it, is presented to research as a series of problems defined by the linkage of its various spheres.

---

[4] This is the case with Chinese reproductions of the *Devils of Ocumichu,* the Huichol designs on luxury clothing by Pineda-Covalín and Paulina and Malinali, or the Mixteca paintings shown on Converse tennis shoes.

[5] These deal with the relationship between climate change and living beings.

5.8 The Sociopolitical Approach to Culture

One of the questions about how to study intangible cultural heritage concerns other strategies that have emerged in the global scenario, such as that presented in the Alliance of Civilizations project.[6]

The question that arises is how the phenomena of gender and racial discrimination and religious intolerance that are the concern of the research foundations of the *United Nations Alliance of Civilizations* (UNAOC) affect the possibility of correctly identifying and recognizing, as well as safeguarding, the cultural heritage of countries and peoples.

The 2003 UNESCO Convention does not visualize cultural heritage from a perspective of sociopolitical and geopolitical interculturality. Many different factors affect both cultural heritage and the laboratory vision of it—an ascetic vision—, and there are many analyses that should reposition themselves within this framework. It should not be forgotten that heritage is understood as something transmitted, and previously determined, by economic processes mediated by power. It is a controversial matter (Zendejas 2012) that is conceived in different ways, depending on the historical situation, the scenario, and the social players. These are fields in which contradictions and different perceptions of the subjects at all levels play a leading role.

Beyond the political relevance that the Alliance of Civilizations project may have, consideration should be given to anthropological research into intangible cultural heritage having to take into account a geopolitical dimension. From this perspective, the very notion of culture has been criticized (Abu Lughod 1991), and this perspective also involves and is influenced by intangible heritage.

How can these phenomena be recognized and studied at an appropriate level from the perspective of intangible cultural heritage? How can it be recognized that there is a framework and a metacultural scenario from which a position is taken, questions are asked, and the significance of culture and heritage brought into play, as, for example, with particular customary concepts, traditions and practices?

Nevertheless, there are difficulties of compatibility that must be overcome between the activity and objectives of anthropological research, on the one hand, and certain legal-regulatory principles concerning cultural heritage, established by the Conventions, on the other. It is no longer a question of there being a scientific tradition as well as a hermeneutic tradition that can diverge from each other, as occurs in the case of anthropology, and between the dynamic of cultural change and legal-regulatory principles. In the first place, this is because regulatory principles usually develop irregularly in time and lag behind sociocultural changes,

---

[6] This project has been promoted in UNESCO by the government of Rodríguez Zapatero (with support from the government of Barack Obama) to promote what might be considered the cultural front of a geopolitical strategy towards the Muslim countries, in keeping with the concept propounded by Samuel Huntington that seeks a rapprochement between cultures rather than a clash.

and in the second place, there is the problem of translating and achieving compatibility between anthropological categories and regulatory categories, since anthropology is a descriptive discipline and legal science is of a nomothetic nature.

In the third place, it is because coincidences and divergences occur in the relationship between the critical-analytic position of anthropology and the ethical and regulatory position of international organizations. Even for a particular anthropological vision, proposals about cultural heritage can appear to be a hegemonic legal-ideological discourse and a new way of attempting once again to typify the *Other*, under the dominant categories. The Weberian separation between what is scientific and what is political reappears in a scheme in which the antonymic polarities are recomposed: between the scientific-comprehensive posture of anthropology and the ethical–political posture of organizations such as UNESCO.

It is not to be expected that anthropology can define a homogeneous ethical posture corresponding precisely to the liberal concepts and principles permeating international organizations. There will surely be tensions concerning certain topics and problems: at every moment, solutions must be sought for these, as a function of new challenges towards which positions are to be adopted, measures taken and ethical-paradigmatic alternatives offered; an example would be issues surrounding what is culturally legitimate and ethical from a Western perspective, but not from others.

Anthropological research can contribute to providing vitality for renewing the concepts, frameworks and regulatory conditions of national and international institutions, and it can exert an influence that may lead to more efficacious actions. There is no doubt that by placing oneself in the perspective of cultural heritage, one finds oneself in the situation of facing a broader concept of research. Such research needs to be applied in a multilateral sense, together with action in the field, linked in a more direct social sense to social management and committed to safeguarding certain practices.

5.9 Emerging Fields and Topics for Research

In the scenario presented, certain topics for research emerge, such as the following:

- Emerging fields for study, such as the heritage of biocultural diversity,[7] about which there is a need to develop the pertinent concepts. In this regard, a form of classification of knowledge has emerged: *Kosmos, Corpus* and *Praxis* in which

---

[7] The project on *Etnografía de las Regiones Indígenas* [Ethnography of Indigenous Regions] under the direction of Eckart Boege and Narciso Bassol through the *Coordinación Nacional de Antropología* [National Coordination of Anthropology] of the *Instituto Nacional de Antropología e Historía* [INAH; National Institute of Anthropology and History] develops a line on *Biocultural Heritage* in which the objective is to establish the relevance of this overall field.

there is an attempt at an encounter and coincidence between the vernacular and scientific forms of conceptualizing.

- A topic related to biocultural diversity from the symbolic and holistic perspective that re-emerges is that of geosymbolic territory and sacred sites. The interest in it comes in large measure from the movements currently manifested in the indigenous regions of the Americas towards resacralization and defence of territories with biodiversity resources. Also engaged in this are the scholars who adopt a systemic vision (for example, the contributions of Arturo Escobar and Bruno Latour). But there are those, such as Peter Sloterdijk, who propose a different relationship to nature, one that takes into account the need to transit from a form of *alotechnological* relationship (instrumental with regard to the world) to another *homeotechnological* relationship (Sloterdijk 2006).
- Cultural heritage in situations along borders or in boundary areas of various types. This is the case of the cultural heritage of migrants and cultural hybridizations. Aspects and moments that are 'blurred and in a sequence of linkages in fragments and pieces of dichotomic representations' (as indicated by Hiernaux 2001: 30, 40). An example is what occurs between countries or the blurring that is manifested in the territorial sphere: the existence of a component of biodiversity with the attributes given to the culture and another symbolic-cultural component with the efficacy of the properties of the former.
- Traditional medicine or ethno-knowledge that is integrated into institutional systems. In another field, there is historical memory, such as the case of memory sites (and this does not appear as such in the classification of the 2003 Convention).
- Concepts and representations of the body and identity (the concept of person).
- The interpretation of the character of the processes of innovation. The heritage that is inscribed in the dynamics of extra-community and global transformation (for example, contemporary indigenous art or regional musical expressions that are projected as new genres (for example, a part of the *son* from Veracruz, in the case of Mexico).
- Research into conceptualization and similarities between fields. For example, in the definition of cognitive units for cultural analysis between the codes of music and language.
- But also research into what is known as conceptual hermaphroditism.[8] For example, practical knowledge[9] (Sennett 2008) and the scope of concepts such as performativity (which involves improvisation and code patterns), or those that refer to transitional situations and shared domains.

---

[8] Günther Gotthart proposes in his transclassic and polycontextual logic that constructions such as signs, machines, works of art, tools, and communications media are hermaphrodites, having an intellectual component and a material component (androgynous in itself).

[9] Also, *implicit knowledge*.

- Concepts that recognize atypical linkages and synergies; for example, in cultural transmission (Déléage 2009).[10] This would be the case for dynamic structures in which the terms of causality are inverted; and forms of recursiveness, as well as the participation of a diversity of physical supports and/or simultaneous spaces in which a cultural phenomenon is expressed.

5.10 Proposals for Possible Lines of Work by the Commission on Heritage

- Demonstrate various areas in which anthropological and ethnological studies can add to knowledge and contribute tools for achieving a better understanding and safeguarding of intangible cultural heritage.
- Obtain a panorama of research projects (and the most important topics) that have been initiated or undertaken in various countries on intangible cultural heritage. Learn about the fields they cover and their objectives and contents in order to evaluate the current status of research in this field.
- Obtain a profile of the evaluation made of the factors and agents that most affect intangible cultural heritage in various regions, countries, and settings.
- Learn about research projects and balances that have been carried out on the various ways of preserving and safeguarding intangible cultural heritage. (Learn about advances such as those made by organizations such as CRESPIAL in South America.)
- Promote research into the importance of secular forms of informal transmission of knowledge and, in particular, traditional knowledge.
- Promote research into the role of languages as a condition for preserving and safeguarding intangible cultural heritage.
- Learn about the panorama and perspectives for safeguarding intangible cultural heritage in view of the accelerated changes caused by globalization and mercantilization of culture in the current era.
- Identify the challenges and characterization of the obstacles faced in the regions, including the efforts to preserve and safeguard intangible cultural heritage.
- Delve more deeply into the various aspects offered by and that characterize cultural diversity (qualities that are favourable to safeguarding intangible cultural heritage) and that contribute towards counteracting the features of cultures that represent an integrist and exclusionary vision.

---

[10] These are unwritten forms of cultural transmission, and there are at least three of them. Pierre Déléage refers to non-intuitive cultural knowledge (what is learned without having been taught); mythological knowledge; and ritual knowledge.

- Increase knowledge of the relationships between innovation and tradition and between change and cultural continuity that are accentuated by globalization.
- Publicize the new fields and manifestations that open up for research into cultural heritage, such as biocultural heritage.

5.11 For a Network of Researchers

Through the network, foster communications and the formation of interdisciplinary teams of researchers from various countries to explore the topics chosen and study them in depth. For example,

- The role of intangible cultural heritage in the new world scenario of culture.
- The importance of intangible cultural heritage in the formulation of sustainability alternatives.
- The importance of traditional knowledge in contexts of innovation and research into alternatives for the linkage of cultural systems, towards the *pluralism of cultural systems of knowledge.*

References

Abu Lughod, Lila, 1991: "Writing Against Culture", in: Fox, Richard (Ed.): *Recapturing Anthropology. Working in the Present* (Santa Fe: School of American Research Press).

Appadurai, Arjún, 2001: *La Modernidad Desbordada: dimensiones culturales de la globalización* (Buenos Aires: Fondo de Cultura Económica).

Briones, Fernando, 2011: "Saberes y Prácticas Climáticas de los Pueblos Indígenas de México: los Choles", in: *Ichan Tecolotl*, 246.

Choay, Françoise, 1992: *L'allégorie du Patrimoine* (Paris: Seuil).

Déléage, Pierre, 2009: "Epistemología del Saber Tradicional", in: *Dimensión Antropológica*, 46.

Florescano, Enrique, (comp) 1993: *El Patrimonio Cultural de México* (México: Fondo de Cultura Económica).

Gorz, André, 2003a: *La Aritmética del Capitalismo Cognitivo. Cerebros al Trabajo. II Manifesto.*

Gorz, André, 2003b: *L'immatériel. Connaissance, valeur et capital* (Paris: Galilée).

Habermas, Jürgen, 1968: *Technik und Wissenschaft als 'Ideologie' La Ciencia y la Tecnología como Ideología* (Madrid: Tecnos). (Spanish translation by Manuel Jiménez Redondo, 1986).

Hiernaux, J. Pierre, 2001: "El Pensamiento Binario. Aspectos Semánticos, Teóricos y Empíricos", in: *Recherches Sociologiques*, XXXII: 25–37 (Spanish translation by Gilberto Giménez in: *Epistemología* 6, 2009).

Sennett, Richard, 2008: *Craftsman* (New Haven: Yale University Press).

Sloterdijk, Peter, 2006: *El Hombre Operable. Notas sobre el estado ético de la tecnología Génica.* at: <http://www.observacionesfilosoficas.net/download/hombreoperable.pdf>

Zendejas Romero, Sergio, 2012: "*Patrimonialización: Contenciosos Procesos de Formación de Objetos Culturales, Colectividades e Identidades Sociales*", Paper for the 3rd National Congress on the Social Sciences, Mexico City.

Chapter 6
New Directions in the Study of Cultural Transmission

David Berliner

Cultural transmission is a hot topic today. The process through which something *'is being passed on from one generation to another'* (Treps 2000, p. 362), it contributes to the creative persistence of representations, practices, emotions and institutions in the present. However, nowadays it is mostly understood through its so-called 'crisis'. I have heard so many times in the field, in West Africa first and more recently at UNESCO meetings, these nostalgic longings about cultural loss and forgetting, the necessity and the impossibility of transmitting. All over the globe, "discourses of the vanishing" (Ivy 1995) lament the disappearance of societies, forms of life, values, identities, roots, languages and so forth. This phenomenon is what I call the contemporary *tout-perdre* (losing everything), which manifests itself through the use of formulations such as 'we lose our culture', 'we have abandoned our customs', 'traditions are vanishing', 'there is nothing left of the past here', often referring to a specific posture vis-à-vis a past seen as irreversible, a set of publicly displayed discourses, practices, and emotions where the ancient is somehow glorified, without necessarily implying the experience of first-hand nostalgic memories. Interestingly, Appadurai has coined the term 'armchair nostalgia' (Appadurai 1996, p. 78) to describe such vicarious nostalgia, observable, for instance, in the attachment of Western tourists and heritage experts to other people's cultural loss (especially in postcolonial worlds, for which Rosaldo's notion of 'imperialist nostalgia' (1989) is also pertinent). Indeed, the trope of the vanishing, key of many tourist attractions (Graburn 1995), is at the core of the philosophy of contemporary preservation policies. And UNESCO, although its perspectives are much more fragmented than one might expect (between different delegations and regional offices), significantly contributes to the dissemination of such nostalgic views about cultural loss around the

D. Berliner (✉)
Laboratoire d'Anthropologie des Mondes Contemporains, Université Libre de Bruxelles–
Institut de Sociologie, Avenue Jeanne, 44-CP124 1050 Brussels, Belgium
e-mail: David.Berliner@ulb.ac.be

L. Arizpe and C. Amescua (eds.), *Anthropological Perspectives on Intangible*
Cultural Heritage, SpringerBriefs in Environment, Security, Development and Peace 6,
DOI: 10.1007/978-3-319-00855-4_6, © The Author(s) 2013

world. The intangible cultural heritage (ICH) paradigm itself is an institutionalized response to such worldwide diagnosis of 'crisis in cultural transmission'.

For anthropologists, as I will show in this chapter, there is a great deal to be researched in these laments about loss, about the vanishing of the *'breath of air which was among that which came before'* (to use Walter Benjamin's phrase) that we keep hearing about in the field. Ethnographies of transmission and loss are still scarce. Whilst ritual, material culture, sexuality or transnationalism are well-established fields of study, cultural transmission and its workings rarely constitute a starting point for research. I see the following pages as a theoretical contribution to a more insightful understanding of how to study cultural transmission—its discourses, practices and mechanisms. I want to argue that for scholars interested in ICH, there must be new theoretical directions to better explore its workings.

6.1 An Old Question and Its Persistence

Anthropology has always been concerned with the retention of the past, the persistence of cultural items and the transmission of forms, the maintenance of social order, the resilience of cognitive structures and the reproduction of symbolic systems. From Tylorian survivals (these "remains of crude old culture which have passed into harmful superstition" (Tylor 1994b, p. 410) which constituted evidences of the "permanence of culture" (Tylor 1994a, p. 63)), the history of our discipline is haunted by the question of cultural transmission and continuity, the problem of the persistence of the past into the present. Indeed, most classical definitions of culture are associated with the notions of transmission and learning, from Herskovits (1956) and Linton (1945) to Geertz (1973). At the same time, on the French side, the notion of tradition played a similar epistemic role as it helped theorists think through continuity and the perpetuation of culture, from Mauss (1950) to Bastide (1970) whose researches investigated how practices re-enact, modify and conserve 'pastness' through time. In the 1950s, Evans-Pritchard also emphasized, in a Durkheimian style, how social facts

> are characterized by [...] their transmissibility [...]. All members of a society have, in general, the same habits and customs, language, and morals [...]. All these things form a more or less stable structure which persists in its essentials over great periods of time, being handed down from one generation to another (Evans-Pritchard 1951, p. 52)

whilst Radcliffe-Brown suggested that

> one of the fundamental theoretical problems [...] is that of the nature of social continuity (Radcliffe-Brown 1952, p. 10).

Although anthropological discourses now seem to have shifted from permanence to rupture, crisis and major social change, I argue that anthropology is still a "science of continuity" (Robbins 2007). Anthropologists are nowadays inclined to see all over the globe societies that are persistent, yet transformed, beyond historical trauma and rupture. Beyond important societal changes and subsequent losses, scholars, even when they wager on rupture, are "longing for continuity in a fragmented world" (Boym 2001, p. xvi), a world of persistent indigenousness in disrupted times. Such a "cult of persistence" manifests itself through a copious use of notions such as memory (Berliner 2005b), resurgence, revival, reinvention, resilience, syncretism, invented traditions, heritage, *habitus* or neo-traditionalism. All these notions imply continuity with the past and give scholars the opportunity to consider the persistence of their objects of study—that is, the reproduction of societies through time, the continuity of representations, practices, emotions and institutions, despite dramatic changes in context. So many contemporary ethnographies demonstrate how 'indigenous' practices and beliefs are still alive and how people create continuities in turbulent times. And, for some, even forgetting and loss are considered as markers of continuity. For instance, Battaglia writes that "forgetting gives rise to society" (Battaglia 1993, p. 430) and, by virtue of its "persistent non-presence" (ibid, p. 438, my emphasis), it serves to prolong "a unitary perdurable social order" (ibid, p. 430). Well, such paradigmatic inclination toward persistence should not come as a surprise. Historically, the social sciences, and anthropology in particular, have been skewed toward describing and explaining retention and continuity (Latour 2006), a perspective shared by cognitive anthropologists (following Sperber and Boyer) who nowadays study the neurological mechanisms that promote the persistence and the transmission of certain mental concepts (Bloch 2005).

6.2 The Practicalities of Cultural Transmission

As much as the question of cultural transmission is foundational to the anthropological project itself, one observes a relative lack of interest in the lived experience and the complex processes which render such operation possible. Many scholars work on the assumption that culture is what is transmitted, and they go no further, implying that, for some, this terrain is reserved to psychologists. The anthropology of education and psychological anthropology have been rather marginal. It also took quite a long time for children to become proper subjects of research for anthropologists. As early as 1938, Meyer Fortes noted that "a great deal of information has been accumulated about what is transmitted from one generation to the next [...]. Of the process of education—how one generation is 'moulded' by the superior generation, how it assimilates and perpetuates its cultural heritage—much less is known" (Middleton 1970, p. 14). Even so, Margaret Mead (1930) paved the way for the anthropology of childhood and ethnographies of learning. Inspired by research into bardic performances, Goody (1977) showed that there is no fixed model for transmission, but rather emphasized the creative and flexible conditions of learning. Later on, *Socialization, Education* or *Learning Studies* were developed by Jean Lave (Lave and Wenger 1991), Solon Kimball and Harry Wolcott, whose texts were mostly published in the relatively peripheral *Anthropology and Education Quarterly*. On the francophone side, since the 1970s,

there has been a growing literature about the transmission of naturalist, professional, religious and musical knowledge (Bromberger 1986, Chevallier 1991).
However rich, this literature is fragmented and has little paradigmatic ambition. I
want to argue that for scholars interested in ICH, there must be new theoretical
ways to grasp the workings of cultural transmission.

Here are two directions that I have taken in my own research over the last ten
years, first in West Africa (Guinea) and now in South East Asia (Laos). First of all,
it may be helpful to distinguish between two levels of analysis: what can be called
the 'reflexive theory of transmission' (the way people perceive and verbalize the
process of transmission and loss itself) and the observable 'processes of transmission' through which knowledge, emotions, and practices are *actually* passed
down. The first level opens onto a fascinating question for anthropologists: what
'transmission' and 'loss' are for people themselves. All over the globe, evidence
suggests that cultural transmission and loss have become politicized issues, as the
concepts are primarily used by politicians, local elites, UNESCO experts and some
anthropologists. The trope of the 'disappearing culture' is also deployed by
ordinary men and women in a world seen by many as globalizing and uprooting. In
various societies, however, UNESCO's naturalist project of collecting and preserving does not correspond to the way cultural transmission and loss are conceived by locals. In the Guinean coastal villages where I have conducted
fieldwork, most elders do perceive a 'crisis in transmission' as masculine initiation
practices (which took place before the 1950s) have been shunned and replaced by
Islam. But, firstly, the coming of Islam is always positively evaluated by them.
And, secondly, this does not in any way imply that elders are willing to pass on
customary non-Islamic knowledge. For them, transmitting knowledge related to
the time of custom, the ancient time before Islam, is considered a loss of their
power, and the preservation of knowledge by a non-initiate is seen as a real threat
to the inherently secret nature of custom. By contrast, unlike the old men who
'abandoned custom' in the 1950s, young people seem greatly concerned about the
passing on of non-Islamic religion today. They do not, however, perceive a 'crisis
in transmission' as described through the lens of Western ideas of cultural
objectification and preservation. Rather, their desire to preserve their non-Islamic
religious heritage is related to the shaping of their collective identity in forming
Guinean postcoloniality and it is, first and foremost, constrained by their fathers'
epistemology of secrecy (Berliner 2005a). Similarly, in my current research in
Luang Prabang in Laos, a town which became a UNESCO World Heritage Site in
1995, I found that the way most inhabitants speak about permanence and loss does
not match the sense of loss expressed by international experts, Lao elites, Western
expatriates and travellers. For instance, I have been struck by how little elderly
people as well as most of the younger generation do actually complain about the
possible vanishing of rituals and the demolition of traditional houses, which have
now become metaphors of cultural loss for UNESCO experts, expatriates and local
politicians. Although alarmist discourses are circulated more and more through
campaigns, many residents of Luang Prabang insist rather on cultural persistence,
emphasizing that they are "keeping on with tradition. Tradition is not changing".

In fact, interviews with locals revealed that they do not long for the return of what seems to some foreign experts and tourists lost for ever, and that they do not share many of the traits of their cultural alarmism (Berliner 2012).

These two examples invite us to take into serious account the way people perceive and verbalize the process of transmission and loss itself. But, whilst peoples hold their own experiences and theories of transmission, anthropologists set up models of what they think 'actually' happens, sometimes highlighting the discrepancy that can exist between peoples' interpretations and scholarly models. Often, the scene for cultural transmission works behind people's objectifications and considerations. In most instances, individuals are being acted on by implicit transmission processes which they creatively engage with habitually without thinking about them explicitly. My research in Guinea has shown that contrary to what village elders say—that transmission is impossible—intergenerational transmission of information about the past 'time of custom' occurs despite the absence of visible objects and ancient rituals. The question is therefore: as anthropologists, how can we describe cultural transmission? How can we identify these processes through which knowledge, emotions, and practices are passed down? How can we grasp such ungraspable reality (usually not grasped by our interlocutors themselves)? Where does cultural transmission start? Are we able to describe it 'in the making' or can we approach it through its effects only? Here, I want to list six some thoughts for further research:

1. Studying cultural transmission is a theoretical posture. Most importantly, exploring it requires that one acknowledges that concepts, practices and emotions from the past do not suddenly 'happen' in people. It entails that one looks for the long processes through which these things circulate between generations and peers, being appropriated by individuals who *actively* acquire them in situations (Lave and Wenger 1991).

2. Cultural transmission *as a theoretical question* nurtures a reflection upon the continuity of human societies in the face of the ruptures of history, and thus necessitates interdisciplinary approaches (sociology, cognitive psychology, biology, memory studies, psychoanalysis, history, archaeology, etc.).

3. To explore the workings of cultural transmission (I would say, the 'chain of transmission'), one needs to track what Bruno Latour calls its 'mediations': protagonists, institutions, gestures, interactions, places, ideologies, critical moments, smells, texts, silences, ordinary moments, sounds, emotions, objects and technologies. In the *longue durée*, the anthropologist researches the media, the contexts, the types of actors, the emotional triggers, the mental processes, the interactions, the communicative facts and the materialities which render such operation of passing down possible. Who transmits what and how? In which social networks, forms of organization and ideologies has such heritage been handed down? Are these processes gendered? What are the sites and the generational contexts in which they take place? Are words and objects the most powerful instruments of transmission?

4. Transmission is not always where we think it is. This leads me to make an observation about the subtle mechanisms at play in cultural transmission. As

Bourdieu (1977) found in Kabyle society, not all transmission is informed by expressed and explicit prescriptions. Rather, every society is constituted through processes of transmission 'that go without saying'. These linguistic interjections or silences, these emotional expressions, these seemingly insignificant gestures, tones, and actions in daily interactions act on individuals and contribute, often implicitly, to instilling "a whole cosmology, an ethic, a metaphysic, a political philosophy" (Bourdieu 1977, p. 94).

5. The scene of cultural transmission is historical—and it is thus not linear. My concern here is about the entanglement of cultural transmission and time. As a matter of fact, cultural transmission takes place within very specific ontological temporalities, which give them their style, possibilities and constraints. Suffice to think of these issues among post-Holocaust diasporic Jews or schismatic Orthodox Old Believers in Romania (Naumescu 2010) who hold their own temporalities for transmission and have particular views on the diagnosis of its crisis. Secondly, the landscape of cultural transmission is itself the result of complex historical processes. As anthropologists, one of our intellectual endeavours consists of resituating the chain of transmission in the midst of such historical contingencies. The result of historical processes, cultural transmission never happens in the same way twice. Passing down is an inherently heterogeneous and creative operation. Failures, blockages, contradictions, inventions, constitute the norm, all of them dimensions which should attract anthropologists' attention. In this regard, it is important for anthropologists interested in ICH to investigate how and why people decide to stop performing cultural practices, or why and how some lose interest in them. Cultural loss as an anthropological conundrum seems to me as revealing as continuity in the study of ICH.

6. Last but not least, cultural transmission is now a global issue. The ICH Convention adopted in Paris at the UNESCO General Assembly in 2003 and implemented by more than 140 States Parties is producing new arrangements of life around the globe, whether social, political, economic or aesthetic (Bortolotto 2011). Indeed, by attempting to preserve cultural practices, UNESCO conventions and experts as well as national heritage professionals, far from inhibiting transmission and culture mechanisms, effectively transform them. Of course, what is getting produced draws on something of the past, but also (re)produces it as something new. This is the performative/transformative reality of UNESCO or what I call 'UNESCOization' (Berliner 2012). This performative reality is obtained through very complex mediations, our role as anthropologists being to describe such mediations.

References

Appadurai, Arjun, 1996: *Modernity at Large. Cultural Dimensions of Globalization* (Minneapolis: University of Minnesota Press).

Bastide, Roger, 1970: "Mémoire collective et sociologie du bricolage", in: *L'Année Sociologique*, 21: 65–108.

Battaglia, Debbora, 1993: "At Play in the Fields (and Borders) of the Imaginary: Melanesian Transformations of Forgetting", in: *Cultural Anthropology*, 8,4: 430–442.

Berliner, David, 2005a: "An 'Impossible' Transmission. Youth Religious Memories in Guinea-Conakry", in: *American Ethnologist*, 32,4: 576–592.

Berliner, David, 2005b: "The Abuses of Memory. Reflections on the Memory Boom in Anthropology", in: *Anthropological Quarterly*, 78,1: 183–197.

Berliner, David, 2012: "Multiple Nostalgias: The Fabric of Heritage in Luang Prabang (Lao PDR)", in: *Journal of the Royal Anthropological Institute*, 18: 769–786.

Bloch, Maurice, 2005: *Essays on Cultural Transmission* (London: Berg Publishers).

Boym, Svetlana, 2001: *The Future of Nostalgia* (New York: Basic Books).

Bortolotto, Chiara, 2011: Le trouble du patrimoine culturel immatériel, in: *Le patrimoine culturel immatériel. Enjeux d'une nouvelle catégorie* (Paris: Editions de la Maison des Sciences de l'Homme).

Bourdieu, Pierre, 1977: *Outline of a Theory of Practice* (Cambridge: Cambridge University Press).

Bromberger, Christian, 1986: "Les savoirs des autres", in: *Terrain*, 6: 3–5.

Chevallier, Denis, 1991: *Savoir-faire et pouvoir transmettre : transmission et apprentissages des savoir-faire et des techniques* (Paris: Editions de la Maison des Sciences de l'Homme).

Evans-Pritchard, Edward, 1951: *Social Anthropology* (London: Cohen and West).

Goody, Jack, 1977: "Mémoire et apprentissage dans les sociétés avec et sans écriture: la transmission du Bagré", in: *L'Homme*, 17,1: 29–52.

Graburn, Nelson, 1995: Tourism, Modernity and Nostalgia, in: Akbar, Ahmed; Chris, Shore, (Eds.): *The Future of Anthropology. Its Relevance to the Contemporary World* (London and Atlantic Highlands: Athlone).

Herskovits, Melville, 1956 (1947): *Man and His Works. The Science of Cultural Anthropology* (New York: Alfred Knopf).

Geertz, Clifford, 1973: *The Interpretation of Cultures. Selected Essays* (New York: Basic Books).

Ivy, Marilyn, 1995: *Discourses of the Vanishing. Modernity, Phantasm, Japan* (Chicago/London: The University of Chicago Press).

Latour, Bruno, 2006: *Changer de société. Refaire de la sociologie* (Paris: Editions de la Découverte).

Lave, J; E, Wenger, 1991: *Situated Learning: Legitimate Peripheral Participation* (Cambridge: Cambridge University Press).

Linton, Ralph, 1945: *The Science of Man in the World Crisis* (New York: Columbia University Press).

Mauss, Marcel, 1950 (1934): *Sociologie et Anthropologie* (Paris: Presses Universitaires de France).

Mead, Margaret, 1930: *Growing up in New Guinea: a Comparative Study of Primitive Education* (New York: W. Morrow & Company).

Middleton, John (ed), 1970: *From Child to Adult. Studies in the Anthropology of Education* (New York: The Natural History Press).

Naumescu, Vlad, 2010: "Le vieil homme et le livre. La crise de la transmission chez les vieux-croyants", in: *Terrain*, 55: 72–89.

Radcliffe-Brown, Alfred, 1952: *Structure and Function in Primitive Society* (London: Cohen and West).

Robbins, Joel, 2007: "Continuity Thinking and the Problem of Christian Culture: Belief, Time, and the Anthropology of Christianity", in: *Current Anthropology*, 48,1: 5–38.

Rosaldo, Renato, 1989: "Imperialist Nostalgia", in: *Representations*, 26: 107–122.

Treps, Marie, 2000: "Transmettre: un point de vue sémantique", in: *Ethnologie Française*, 30,3: 361–367.

Tylor, Edward, 1994a (1871): *Primitive Culture. Research into the Development of Mythology, Philosophy, Religion, Art and Custom*, Vol. 1 (London: Routledge).

Tylor, Edward, 1994b (1871): *Primitive Culture. Research into the Development of Mythology, Philosophy, Religion, Art and Custom*, Vol. 2 (London: Routledge).

Chapter 7
Thoughts on Intangibility and Transmission

Mary Louise Pratt

The concept of intangibility points, among other things, to investigations focused on the workings of *cultural transmission and reproduction.* In contrast with material artefacts, intangible creations endure only through active, socially maintained processes of transmission from older to younger practitioners. These transmissions usually involve training and apprenticeships, sizeable investments of time and energy that must be meaningful and rewarding for this who undertake them. Languages, of course, exist in just this way, and may provide an illuminating paradigm for the transmission of intangible heritage, and for research on that subject (Fig. 7.1).

The linguistic paradigm suggests, for example, a focus not on the cultural creation itself—the particular ritual, cuisine, song form, design—but on the expertise involved, and the ways that expertise is transmitted or reproduced over time. Language acquisition is often regarded as natural and spontaneous, but it is not. Language learning (of first or subsequent languages) requires five things in abundance: time, effort, motivation, input, and opportunities for use. (Literacy requires a sixth, instruction.) Linguistic communities lay down social arrangements and practices that provide those elements. The breakdown of those arrangements is the only way languages can 'die', that is, through the interruption of the circuit of transmission from older to younger speakers. This usually comes about through a drastic disruption of social and material life.

It might be productive to extend this way of thinking to the expressive forms identified as items of intangible heritage. Perhaps the descriptions of these items or instances should include information on how they are transmitted, through what relationships, institutions, pedagogical practices, and value structures. How can these dimensions be built into the concept of intangible heritage? As it stands now, the focus (as ever in modern cultural thought) is on production and the product,

M. L. Pratt (✉)
Department of Social and Cultural Analysis, New York University,
20 Cooper Square, 4th Floor, New York, NY 10003, United States
e-mail: mlp7@nyu.edu

L. Arizpe and C. Amescua (eds.), *Anthropological Perspectives on Intangible Cultural Heritage*, SpringerBriefs in Environment, Security, Development and Peace 6,
DOI: 10.1007/978-3-319-00855-4_7, © The Author(s) 2013

Fig. 7.1 Chinelos at Yautepec's carnival (2009). *Source* Photo by Carolina Buenrostro

and an account of the latter can be experienced as a necessary and sufficient account of the practice.

Once transmission arrangements become part of the object of study, interesting questions arise around practices or knowledges that have stopped reproducing themselves, that is, whose transmission has ceased. What is the ontological status of these objects? In the case of languages, we call them 'dead'. What mode of existence do 'dead' languages have? For the most part the answer would be 'none'. No one has any idea at all of how many human languages have come and gone in the history of humankind. Intangible objects, by definition, can disappear without a trace. Or they can leave traces—shards, ceremonial objects, lexical items, place names, written signs. These can be used in efforts at artificial reconstruction that try to restore, albeit in fragmented, speculative form, the interrupted circuit of transmission, to pick up the broken thread. Consider the Maya glyphs (and the conditions under which they became indecipherable).

Perhaps more pertinent to intangible heritage policies is the category of the 'endangered', a status that motivates many entries on the list. This label marks a call for material investments to strengthen or revitalize a practice and its transmission: subventions for artists, scholarships for learners, contests and prizes, creation of public value, and so on. In other words, interventions are made to restore those five things needed to sustain transmission: time, effort, motivation, input, and opportunities for use. When a practice is perceived to be 'dying', that is, unable to reproduce itself over time, salvage operations come into play. In the case of languages, these take a range of forms. For linguists the priority is to document all the grammatical forms and the lexicon so these can be analysed. Anthropologists focus on recording rituals, stories, oratory, songs—the archive and the repertoire. Both of these involve the conversion of the intangible into tangible materializations—recordings, transcriptions, grammars. This is the passage from live (evolving) transmission to dead (non-evolving) transmission. Of course, materialized 'dead' transmissions can later be used to bring practices back to life—to 'revitalize' intangible creations and place them back into circuits of live transmission. In an Ojibway reservation I know in central Canada, a residential school system interrupted language transmission in the 1940s and 1950s. Today tribal office holders are required to carry MP3 players and listen throughout the day to recordings of native speakers, of whom a handful remain. The goal is for the language to recover its intangible life and its circuit of transmission down the generations. Ethnographers tell stories of tribal leaders consulting written ethnographies to find out how a particular ritual 'should' be done. Is it of interest to think about these possibilities in terms of transmission and reproduction? Are they hybrid processes?

Another process that might be thought of as hybrid transmission involves the *refunctionalizing* of cultural practices, knowledges, or forms. Let me take two items now on the intangible heritage List. In Peru the *'baile de las Tijeras'*, the scissor dance, was already disappearing from Andean village fiestas in the 1960s. Films were made to preserve what was thought to be a disappearing form. Today the scissor dance has resurged as an accompaniment to Andean-infused rock bands that perform all over Peru, and is admired for the same athletic qualities that made it special in village tradition. There are probably more scissor dancers now than there ever were. The Chinese dragon boat has reappeared in North America as a fixture in community festivals where lakes or rivers are involved (Edmonton, Toronto). One is reminded: intangibility gives creations an uncanny ability to **travel**—in fact, they tend to be things that, like languages, *cannot be left behind*, though they can, over time, be forgotten. While the UNESCO List associates particular practices with the nation states whose cultural capital they are, the causal link between intangibility and mobility bears thinking about.

Finally, how can we describe the intervention that entry on the List itself makes? When a dance or a cuisine or a myth becomes an item of intangible heritage, what changes? Does its ontological status shift? Or is it merely a matter of acquiring an expanded existence? Certainly the practice itself is affected. Let me given an entirely unscientific, anecdotal example. I grew up near an Amish village called St Jacobs where a store sold the quilts the women made over the long winter months. After many years away, I returned there to look for a quilt to buy, and found it had become a tourist destination for people from the city (Toronto). The store had become a 'Country Store' where one could buy 'Amish Quilts', and inside the store on the second floor on display sat an Amish woman, quilting. The sight of the woman on display, performing an 'authentic' enactment of quilting shook me to my core. I felt I was in an ontologically altered universe, that a form of being had changed. Perhaps the shift is only epistemological: 'Amish quilt' and 'St Jacobs' had entered new registers of meaning linked to marketing strategies and touristification. An aura had been constructed around the place and woven through it, that was fake for those who'd known it before, and authentic for those who were attracted there now. The key term here I believe is performance or performativity, or perhaps performability. Once there is a list, the intangible items or practices or knowledges on it become performable, that is, they can be articulated as performances addressed to spectators—as the Day of the Dead in Tzintzunzan attracts tens of thousands of spectators from Mexico City. Does inclusion in the List produce changes that are consistent across cases? To what extent can these changes be summed up as commodification? And to what extent not? When performability comes into play, how does transmission change? How does the life form mutate?

Chapter 8
Intangible Cultural Heritage Policy in Japan

Shigeyuki Miyata

8.1 The Dynamics of Intangible Cultural Heritage in Japan

At present, three categories of ICH are protected by the national government of Japan.

The first, "intangible cultural property", is the best known. This is defined as "drama, music and craft techniques, and other intangible cultural products, which have a high historical or artistic value for Japan".

The second category is "intangible folk cultural properties". This is defined as "manners and customs related to food, clothing, and housing, livelihoods, religious faiths, annual events, folk performing arts, folk techniques, which are indispensable for understanding the transition in the modes of life of Japanese people".

The third category is "preservation techniques for cultural properties". This is defined as "traditional techniques and craftsmanship indispensable for the conservation of cultural properties". These three categories are fundamental to the support of the succession of tangible and intangible culture in Japan.

8.2 Creation of Intangible Cultural Heritage

In Japan, *intangible cultural heritage* (ICH) is conceived as such as soon as it starts to be developed. This is because when it is first created, it is not known whether it will become the cultural heritage only of one particular group or whether it will be shared with others and transmitted to future generations. In other

S. Miyata (✉)
Cheif Specialist for Cultural Properties, Traditional Cultural Division,
Agency for Cultural Affairs, Government of Japan, 3-2-2, Kasumigaseki,
Chiyoda-ku, Tokyo 100-8589, Japan
e-mail: s-miyata@bunka.go.jp

L. Arizpe and C. Amescua (eds.), *Anthropological Perspectives on Intangible Cultural Heritage*, SpringerBriefs in Environment, Security, Development and Peace 6, DOI: 10.1007/978-3-319-00855-4_8, © The Author(s) 2013

Fig. 8.1 Research Planning Meeting on Intangible Cultural Heritage, CRIM–UNAM, Cuerna-vaca, Morelos (2012). *Source* Photo by Carolina Buenrostro

words, only some parts of many cultural practices might survive for a long time and become intangible cultural heritage properly, that is, shared among a broad community as part of their cultural identity.

In each period of history there have been some cases where most of the avant-garde elements (or *subcultural* elements as the younger generation would call it) gradually spread to the whole of society and became a part of Japanese ICH. This is particularly the case with the field of traditional performing arts, rituals and ceremonies. I will give three examples.

8.2.1 Example 1: Nôgaku Theatre

Nôgaku Theatre, which has been proclaimed as one of the Masterpieces of the Oral and Intangible Heritage of Humanity and has been incorporated in the Repre-sentative List of the *Convention for the Safeguarding of the Intangible Cultural Heritage* by UNESCO, is considered today as one of the most important classical performing arts of Japan due to its symbolic and spiritual character. Yet, at the first period of its history, it was called *Sarugaku* and regarded as a contemporary and popular kind of performing art. Compared to another performing art, *gagaku*, which was enjoyed by aristocrats in earlier years, nôgaku was thought to be an art belonging to the lower class. Later, it was supported by the newly emerging samurai class, and as its artistic character was refined and became stylized, it began to be recognized as one of the classical forms of the performing arts. In the modern period, Nôgaku Theatre was given the status of intangible cultural heritage.

8.2.2 Example 2: Kabuki Theatre

The Kabuki Theatre, now regarded as an important part of Japanese classical drama, was once thought to be a very avant-garde and popular rather than classical performing art. In fact, the word *kabuki* comes from the old verb *kabuku*, which meant to shock other people by strange appearance and behaviour. In the late sixteenth and early seventeenth centuries, young people dressed in such odd costumes and behaving in such an abnormal way that adults felt uneasy were referred as *kabuki-mono*, literally 'kabuki-man'. They might be compared with today's metal or punk youngsters. In its early days, the Kabuki Theatre incorporated this contemporary popular culture of the younger generation into the dance and the drama, and for this reason, the theatrical play was named *kabuki*.

We still find these aspects today in the actors' way of dressing and using make-up. In earlier times, Kabuki Theatre was performed mainly by women and they also wore the costume of *kabuki-mono*, so that Kabuki Theatre represented the fashion of those days. Later, the Tokugawa shogunate banned actresses from the Kabuki Theatre, yet from the seventeenth to the nineteenth century it kept its status as a contemporary performing art and was frequently presented in the outside world. However, in the twentieth century, new kinds of performing arts influenced by Western theatrical performances developed and became popular, and people recognized Kabuki Theatre as one of the classical performances, and so today it is considered as intangible cultural heritage.

8.2.3 Example 3: Dengaku

Broadly speaking, Dengaku refers to folk performing arts related to agricultural celebrations. That is, it includes *Ta-asobi* and *Taue-odori*, the practice of praying for a rich harvest by enacting the annual process of farming. It includes *Hayashi-da*, the musical accompaniment to actual rice planting for the healthy growth of the crop, and *Dengaku* in its narrower sense, which was mainly played by older professional Buddhist performers as it is known today.

Its origin is not known, yet one possible reason for its wide dissemination around the country is that it became the most fashionable event and performance, and was very popular among townspeople. In the late eleventh century, it became even more popular among people in Kyoto, regardless of class. Today, according to historical documents, we can find aristocrats who at that time noted these events in their diaries with great enthusiasm. Thereafter, professional performers who were Buddhist monks began to take part, and the performance became more varied. Soon after, however, Nôgaku Theatre became more popular in urban areas, and Dengaku gradually became out of date. Yet it kept its popularity in rural areas as it was integrated and adopted into regional agricultural practices. That is why Dengaku is still seen today as intangible cultural heritage.

8.3 The Creation of Intangible Cultural Heritage in the Modern Period

These examples are all from the nineteenth century or earlier. Is it then possible to find similar processes in modern history as well?

The modernization of Japan, as of many other non-Western countries, began with its encounter with Western civilization. As a result, in the cultural sphere, Japan has always struggled with the merging of and the conflict between the culture which originally existed in Japan and that imported from the West. Generally speaking, after the Meiji Restoration in 1868, the younger generation preferred the culture of Western countries and paid little attention to creating new cultural practices based on the traditions of their own country.

About 150 years after the Restoration, the situation has changed: there are some cultural phenomena where traditional aspects are mixed with contemporary elements.

One of these examples is today's trend for Yosakoi-style festivals. These are festivals that have been newly developed and that are based on the Yosakoi festival of the Kochi area in Japan, and in this first decade of the twenty-first century, we can find many versions all over the country.

8.4 The Yosakoi Festival of Kochi Prefecture

The Yosakoi festival of Kochi prefecture is more than half a century old, as it began in 1954. The festival was originally organized by the local Tourism Division of the Chamber of Commerce and Industry. The festival was started by people motivated by the big summer festival in the prefecture adjacent to Kochi, the Awa dance festival in Tokushima. They wanted to have as large a scale festival as Tokushima's. Then it became so popular that it is now recognized as the *must* summer event for Kochi. Today, the festival is supported mainly by groups of young people who regard it as an occasion to show off the creativity of their dances. Originally, there were only 700 people in twenty teams, but now there are about 20,000 participants in 200 teams.

One of the crucial reasons for Yosakoi's popularity today lies in its flexible rules. Most of the traditional festivals of Japan have strict rules about who can join, how they dress, what kind of music is to be used, how those taking part may dance and so on. Organizers make it difficult for the younger generation to experiment with their imagination and creativity. In contrast, Yosakoi festival has very simple rules:

- the use of *naruko* instruments (similar to castanets) played with the hands, and stepping forward in the dance;
- the insertion of some phrases from an old local folk song '*Yosakoi naruko odori*' into the music;
- one team may consist of about 150 members;
- the size of the bandwagon (*jikata-sha*) for the music players should be no more than 8.5 m in length and 3.8 m in height.

These are the only four rules which participants should follow. In other words, within these four rules they are then free to develop their own ideas about costumes, ways of dancing, and arrangements of the music they use. Moreover, in real festivals, there are competitions among participating teams, and that stimulates their creative mind. We must keep in mind that within this *freedom* under the rules, the use of *naruko* traditional castanets and local folk song are compulsory. This reminds us of the continuity between local tradition and contemporary transformation, and so Yosakoi plays an important role as a new festival in the community.

Since its first appearance, over 50 years have passed, and now the festival forms a part of the cultural identity of the community. In the near future, it might well be recognized as an important aspect of intangible cultural heritage in the Kochi area. In that sense, we are witnessing the very moment of creation of a new aspect of intangible cultural heritage.

8.5 The Yosakoi Soran Festival in Sapporo

Another important aspect of the Kochi festival is that it has an impact beyond its geographical area: Yosakoi is now enjoyed by many more people all over the country. One of the early examples of Yosakoi played outside Kochi is the Yosakoi Soran Festival in Sapporo, which is even more popular than Kochi's original.

Sapporo's Yosakoi was started by a university student of the city who saw the Kochi Yosakoi and was moved by its unique character. He liked it and began planning to organize a similar festival in his home town, Sapporo. The first Yosakoi Soran Festival was held in June 1992. Later on, the festival attracted more and more people, and today, more than 30,000 participants and 200,000 spectators gather for the occasion. It is one of the largest festival events in Japan. Sapporo's Yosakoi is as simple as Kochi's. That is, it has the following elements:

- the use of *naruko* castanets;
- the insertion of phrases from the old local folk song '*Soran-bushi*' into the music;
- one team may consisted of about 150 members;

- each team's performance lasts for less than four and a half hours;
- the size of the bandwagon (*jikata-sha*) for the music players should be no more than 9.5 m in length, 2.5 m in width and 3.8 m in height.

Sapporo's Yosakoi Soran is basically the same as Kochi's in that participants have great freedom in composing their music and dances and making their costumes. They may also use more than one phrase from the local folk song.

8.6 A New Form of Expression of Tradition: Cosplay

The Yosakoi Festival and Yosakoi Soran Festival are good examples of the traditional idea of a festival that is reinterpreted in a contemporary style. Another new form of expression in the field of subculture that is interesting is the contemporary practice of *Cosplay*.

In the field of popular culture and subculture Japanese animation is very popular today, but until recently it has been considered that it has nothing to do with the country's cultural traditions. Rather, educated adults have tended to despise anything related to animation as *otaku* culture, or culture belonging to only a few people. In particular, so-called *cosplay*, the abbreviated word for 'costume-play', where participants are disguised as their favourite characters in television programmes or video games, has been ignored. Looking back on the history of festivals and performing arts, however, this has been often the case: in the Edo period, on festive occasions, people would celebrate the event while dressed in the costume of heroes and other characters in popular stories. Today's *cosplay* plays a similar role in society in the sense that young people try to experience the world from the perspective of their heroes and heroines. Disguising oneself is the traditional Japanese way to express such a desire.

Of course, not all popular cultural expressions will survive and be transmitted to the future. Yet we should keep in mind that any of today's subcultures may be the intangible cultural heritage of tomorrow if we look to examples from the past: Kabuki was not accepted by more mature audiences at first, but today it is recognized as part of the intangible cultural heritage of Japan. Therefore, it is essential to foster new forms of cultural expressions even though they might be considered unacceptable and unfavourable at first.

In this first section, I have discussed the trend in cultural expressions which were at first not considered the intangible cultural heritage of Japan but were later recognized as such. I have also discussed how important fostering new cultural expression is to the future development of ICH. To conclude, I would like to summarize some key points of the creation and development of intangible cultural heritage for future research.

In order for a new intangible cultural heritage to be created, any popular cultural expression should keep on developing until it is socially recognized as a tradition. To endure in time, transmission to the next generation is crucial.

Generally speaking, in Japanese history it is after three generations that a cultural expression comes to be regarded as a tradition. In other words, it takes a long time to become a part of cultural identity in this society, but this may also be the case in other societies.

It takes a longer period for cultural expressions that are completely foreign to domestic culture to be widely disseminated in Japan. Indeed, there were some cases such as Buddhism or *kanji* Chinese characters which originally came from China and the Korean peninsula a 1000 years before they were widely disseminated. It took hundreds and perhaps even thousands of years for Japanese people to recognize them as their own culture. Today, we live in a world of rapid information and the influence of Western culture arrives in every place from every corner of the world with only a slight delay. In this situation, cultures from outside tend to remain 'foreign' to domestic people until they are updated before being reinterpreted and becoming a part of people's cultural identity. In this sense, any new cultural expression should have something to do with some existing cultural tradition in order to become intangible cultural heritage in the future. This is particularly important for Japan as a non-Western country.

Intangible cultural heritage is a cultural tradition uniquely constructed in and by a particular community. To ensure the better future of intangible cultural heritage, it is important to pass the heritage on to future generations as well as safeguarding it. The intangible cultural heritage of tomorrow might well exist in today's subcultures. It is particularly the older generations who should keep this in mind and encourage the younger generation's creativity and the birth of new cultural expressions. This will lead to cultural enrichment in the future.

8.7 Documentation of Japanese Intangible Cultural Heritage

It has been 60 years since the Japanese government began to protect its intangible cultural heritage. Various types of documentation have been created in the process and this has resulted in the promotion of the protection of cultural property to some extent.

I will now give an overview of the methods of documenting intangible cultural heritage in Japan (intangible cultural properties, intangible folk cultural properties, and preservation techniques for cultural properties), and introduce the *Guidelines for Visual Documentation of Intangible Folk Cultural Properties* issued by the National Research Institute for Cultural Properties.

8.7.1 Documentation Procedures of Intangible Cultural Heritage in Japan

8.7.1.1 Documentation of Intangible Cultural Properties

Subject: important intangible properties and intangible cultural properties for which documentation and other measures should be taken.

Recorded by: Government, related institutions (National Theatre of Japan, National Research Institute for Cultural Properties, Tokyo).

Documentation method: Written documentation, audio and visual documentation, process sample etc.

Documentation of Performing Arts
Records prepared by the government

- Centring on the Cultural Heritage Preservation Committee, documentation began in 1950 and includes: audio documentation of the background music of Noh, *biwa* music, monochord and other traditional music; documenting of scores for court music and movements for kabuki; and visual documentation of Nogaku, Ningyo Johruri Bunraku (puppet act) and kabuki on 35 mm film.
- With the opening of the National Theatre in 1966, the national documentation projects were replaced with the records of performances at the National Theatre. It is rare for the Agency for Cultural Affairs to engage in any independent documentation project on performing arts.

Documentation prepared by relevant institutions

- All performances at each public facility (Main theatres, National Bunraku Theatre, National Noh Theatre, National Engei hall, National Theatre Okinawa) of the National Theatre of Japan (the Japanese Arts Council, independent administrative entity).
- The Department of Intangible Cultural Heritage, together with the National Research Institute for Cultural Properties, Tokyo, another independent administrative entity, continues to continue independent audio and visual documentation of traditional performing arts.

Documentation of Crafts Arts

- Documentation in the area of crafts arts is basically carried out by the government in the form of written or photographic documentation, samples of the production process involving actual craft items, finished samples, samples of tools used, and documentary films on the production process.
- Written documentation continued until 1970 when it was replaced by one documentary film (35 mm) a year. From 1971 to 2008, thirty-six documentary films were produced.

Issues around Documentation of Intangible Cultural Properties

- Documentation of performing arts, especially for important intangible cultural properties, consists mainly of the record of independent performances at the National Theatre, which is the record of each performance and sometimes lacks programmes and other techniques that should be documented.
- For the performing arts selected as intangible cultural properties for which documentation should be provided and other measures taken, documentation in some form or another has already been produced, but most of this was carried out more than 30 years ago, and any changes since then has not been properly captured. In particular, because of technical limitations at the time of documentation, visual documentation was produced for only a limited number of items.
- At this point, the government, the National Theatre, the National Research Institute for Cultural Properties, Tokyo, and the owner of such properties should get together to review further documentation requirements and implement systematic documentation projects.

8.7.1.2 Documentation of Intangible Folk Cultural Properties

Subject: all intangible folk cultural properties including intangible folk properties unrecognized or unselected by the government.

Recorded by: Government, local public bodies, preservation groups in local communities.

Documentation method: written documentation (reports), visual documentation.

Documentation of Customs and Traditions

- In 1955, the government created the documentation initiatives and has been publishing an 'Annual Intangible Cultural Property Record', with fifty-three annual records published up to 2008.
- For visual documentation, one item of visual documentation has been published in collaboration with the National History-Folk Museum starting from 1984, and public funds are supported for visual documentation projects by local public bodies.

Documentation of Folk Performing Arts

- As for documentation projects initiated by the government, the performance of any artist at the 'National Folk Performing Arts Festival' and 'Regional Folk Performing Arts Festival' which takes place in five regional districts nationwide is documented in writing, in photographs, and in records, and part is published in the 'Documentation of Intangible Cultural Properties: Performing Arts 1–4'.
- Most of the documentation of folk performing arts, however, is led by Japanese municipalities, *shi cho son,* with support from government funds.

Issues with Documentation of Intangible Folk Cultural Properties

- Most documentation projects for intangible folk cultural properties are led by municipalities or preservation groups in local communities of various sizes and with different objectives. The government in principle plays a limited role by providing financial support and operational advice if necessary.
- As many projects have a limited budget and time span, the quality of documentation from them varies depending on the awareness of the person in charge of the project and the quality of the production company. In order to secure visual documentation sufficient to serve the purpose of the conservation of cultural properties, a set of guidelines are required, ranging from planning to actual filming and editing.

8.7.1.3 Documentation of Conservation Techniques for Cultural Properties

- Government protection for conservation techniques for cultural properties is focused on support for training successors to the properties, rather than on systematic documentation. The holders of cultural properties selected by the government, whether a person or an entity, are provided with financial support, and documentation is part of the area of support. Most projects are to nurture a successor and to improve techniques and skills, and few are for documentation.
- Documentation of conservation techniques for cultural properties should be more than a topic in the supplementary meeting, and should be treated as a subject for new type of independent project by the government and related agencies.

8.7.2 Guideline for Visual Documentation of Intangible Folk Cultural Properties

8.7.2.1 The Importance of Visual Documentation in the Safeguarding of Intangible Folk Cultural Properties

Since the early days, much importance has been attached to the recording process as one of the methods for handing down intangible folk cultural properties to posterity. Since it is virtually impossible to preserve an intangible folk cultural property in its original form, preserving it by recording has long been considered to be the next best method and has become the major method for conserving cultural property. And among these recording methods, visual documentation has become the most popular in recent years.

Compared to other recording media, visual images seem to have the most advantages when it comes to documenting intangible cultural properties. For example, visual documentation may be said to be the only means of documentation that is both easily accessible and that is capable of recording intangible folk cultural property manifested through the human body as movements through the passage of time. Visual documentation may also be highly regarded as one of the very few means capable of handing down to posterity the bodily techniques involved in the performing arts and industrial arts, which emphasize bodily skills. Moreover, visual images and their accompanying audio recordings are documentation of extremely high specificity, which, at the same time, offers the opportunity to the general public to replay and appreciate the recordings with relative ease. In terms of its capability of conveying to a wide range of people the image of a cultural property with particular specificity, no one can doubt the effectiveness of the visual image over reports composed from words. Furthermore, visual documentation projects necessarily require a cooperative relationship between the successor (of the cultural property) and the producer. In such a relationship, it is hoped that the successor will recognize the significance of the folk event and find new meaning, thereby bringing new life to the process of handing down tradition. In this way, the making, safekeeping and utilization of visual documentation are considered to be one of the most meaningful projects in conserving intangible folk cultural properties.

This guideline intends to outline the fundamental concepts and procedures involved in the making of visual documentation, particularly as it relates to the administration of cultural property protection, and it assumes that such recordings will be made by those at the forefront of safeguarding intangible folk cultural properties. Visual documentation methods have changed significantly as a result of the recent strides in technological innovations. Yet even more than the technological advances, the making of better quality recordings is dependent on the motivation and the sensitivities of those engaged in the project. Unfortunately, however, there has been little discussion of the methods to date, despite recognition of the significance of visual documentation, and little opportunity for the exchange of information and opinions among those involved. It is hoped that this guideline will be instrumental in raising the awareness of the many who are involved in visual documentation and the materialization of better quality projects.

The contents of this guideline have been compiled based on the results of the deliberations of the *Conference on Creating Visual Documentation of Intangible Folk Cultural Properties* which took place from 2003 to 2007 at the Independent Administrative Institution, National Research Institute for Cultural Properties, Tokyo.

8.7.2.2 Basic Concept Behind the Creation of Visual Documentation

Clarification of purpose

The most important aspect of planning a visual documentation project is to clarify the purpose of creating the documentation. Once the purpose is determined, the type of recording will determine itself and the method of proceeding with the project, the methods for shooting/editing and necessary expenses will also be determined. Moreover, unless the purpose is clear, future plans for the utilization of the documentation cannot be formulated. Clarifying the purpose constitutes the main premise of the project.

The Characteristics of Visual Documentation According to Type

(1) *Visual Documentation for Record Retention*

This type of visual documentation fixes the image of an intangible folk cultural property to a specific point in time and hands it down to posterity. Consequently, when creating this type of document, it is important to try to make a wide-ranging and multifaceted recording that extends to peripheral matters, such as the surrounding environment and conditions, which support the transmission of the folk cultural property. Moreover, in order to enhance its value as documentation, the recording must capture as faithfully as possible the phenomenon at hand, and must always remain objective, even more so than the other types of documentation

(2) *Visual Documentation for Transmission/Successor Training*

This type of visual documentation is made to support the actual transmission of the intangible folk cultural property in the community. For this reason, this type of documentation requires detailed and specific recordings of bodily skills. If necessary, recordings could take place under conditions that are more ideal than those conditions in which the skill is actually practised. Additionally, the cooperation of the successor could be sought and ways could be devised for incorporating information that generally accompanies skills, such as useful hints and the mindset in practising the skill, in the visual documentation.

(3) *Visual Documentation for Publicity/Dissemination*

This type of visual documentation is created in order for it to be seen by as many people as possible and to raise awareness and interest in the viewer, and to eventually lead the viewer to cherish the subject. Unlike the other two, this type of documentation must take into full account its effects on the viewer. For this reason, documentation must be compact and will require ways to make it more easily understood. However, such initiatives should be limited to ways of heightening the audience's understanding of the intangible folk cultural property.

8.7.2.3 Becoming Aware of the Characteristics of the Visual Documentation

Visual documentation has a number of advantages over other types of documentation. One of the greatest advantages is its ability to record and re-create visual images, such as the movements of the body, as successive changes (movements) in time.

However, on the other hand, it must also be remembered that such advantages of the visual image stand side by side with its limitations. Depending on the perspective of the producer, the same subject could appear in a considerably different light and in this sense, it may be said that even visual documentation cannot escape its limitation of representing only a portion of reality, which has been separated under a specific intent.

Therefore, we must not attempt to record 'everything' with visual documentation, but consider what can be most effectively recorded through visual image.

Moreover, to prevent a biased perspective, the participation by people of various positions is essential throughout the project.

8.7.2.4 Ample Preparation in the Pre-production Stage

It is clear by now that when planning visual documentation projects while keeping in the mind the above, advance preparation becomes an extremely important factor. Clarification of the purpose will be required from the initial planning stage. Moreover, in order to reflect a wide range of viewpoints in the documentation, there are a number of roles that the outsourcer, i.e. the organization responsible for the project, must actively take on, such as advance negotiations with the successor, establishing the production committee, explanation of the production policy to the contractor, etc.

In recent developments, heightened awareness is also required for copyright considerations in regard to the completed documentation. In terms of copyright and neighbouring rights (performers' rights), suffice it to say that communication among the related parties is imperative. It is essential that before the project goes into production, the outsourcer carefully explains in advance to the contractor and the successor of the cultural property about the details of the project and makes sure that the significance of the project is understood.

8.7.2.5 Upgrading the System for Retention and Utilization of the Completed Documentation

Some will consider the visual documentation project to be completed once the deliverables are completed or delivered. However, in view of the original purpose of the project, the important thing is that the completed documentation is fully utilized. The assessment of the project will ultimately be linked to how and to what extent the completed documentation is utilized. Consequently, ways must be devised for the documentation to be proactively retained and utilized according to its purpose.

8.7.3 Preparation and Advance Research
for the Development of Visual Documentation

8.7.3.1 The Importance of Preparation and Advance Research

8.7.3.2 The Importance of Researchers

8.7.3.3 The Process of Preparation and Advance Research

Example of preparation and advance research process.

1. Confirmation of the status of transmission and request for cooperation from the community successors (Outsourcer).
2. Formulation of the production guidelines (Outsourcer).
3. Launch of the production committee (Outsourcer/production committee).
4. Preparation of the specifications and public notification (Outsourcer).

The specification sheet should, at least, contain the following items as conditions:
Name of project, the organization responsible for the project
Production period (date of delivery)
Video formats
Advance research period and filming period (number of days)
Form of the finished product (specifications, format, quantity, etc.)
Composition of necessary production/filming staff
Experience requirements for production/filming staff in similar projects
Compliance with copyright laws.

5. Explanation of production guidelines and specifications (Outsourcer/production committee).
6. Preparation of the project proposal (Contractor).
7. Selection of the contractor (Outsourcer/production committee).
8. Meetings with the contractor (Outsourcer/production committee).
9. Preparation of the production schedule (Contractor).
10. Advance research (Outsourcer/production committee/contractor).
11. Preparation of the shooting plan (Contractor).
12. Consideration of the shooting plan (Outsourcer/production committee).
13. Staff meeting (Contractor).
14. Location hunting.

8.7.3.4 Organization of the Production Committee

Specific roles to be played by the production committee could include the following:

- Deliberate on the production guidelines and settle on the production policy
- Give advice on the selection of the contractor
- Deliberate on the shooting plan prepared by the contractor and give advice
- Be present at the advance research and on the shooting/editing site, and express opinions if any, and be there for consultation for the production/filming staff.
- Decide, by the time the tentatively edited work is to be shown in preview, on whether the work in production is following the production policy.
- Confirm that the contents and terminology used in the narrations and the captions are accurate.

8.7.3.5 The Actual Practice of Advancing Research

- The research contents
- Examples of research items for advance research
- From the folklore perspective

  - The origin, the organization responsible for succession, relationship with everyday life
  - Recent status of and changes in succession
  - Current order of the ceremony, progression and required time
  - Name and age of current major successors
  - Preparation and rehearsals
  - The scope of distribution of the succession and similar folk phenomena in the area
  - The day of the festival/observance (e.g. the number of spectators)

- From the technical perspective

  - Confirmation of prohibited locations, and scenes and procedures, which the successor does not wish to be filmed
  - Securing filming location and camera position
  - Scope of movement
  - Sound elements, volume and balance (the volume of the instruments, clapping by the spectators, etc.)
  - Brightness, source of light (when lighting is to be used during the filming, permission should be obtained from the successor)
  - Securing power source
  - Securing a flow line (assuming the movement of spectators)
  - Whether there will be other parties filming
  - The required time for each procedure and performance (taking into account the timing for replacing tape).

8.7.4 Points to Keep in Mind in the Shooting and Editing Process

8.7.4.1 Basic Attitude Toward the Making of Visual Documentation

The two most important mindsets going into the actual filming are summarized below:

- Conduct adequate advance research and get to know the subject well
- Show respect for the folklore which is to be subject of the film, and for the local people.
  On the location site, specific points to be noted are as follows:

  1. Confirm the position for setting up the camera and the flow line in advance and be sure to obtain the consent of the related parties.
  2. With the cooperation of the successor, gain the cooperation of other filming crew and spectators toward the documentation project.
  3. In the case of folk performances of festivals/observances where certain scenes are restricted from being released to the public, a relationship of trust must be maintained with the successor and the question of to what extent scenes can be recorded and released to the public must be dealt with carefully.

8.7.4.2 Filming and Editing Methods

- Method of shooting the film:

  1. Determine the main subject of the film and make sure that the subject in its entirety appears on the screen.
  2. Series of acts/actions must always be filmed with the awareness of their segments and as a flowing series from the beginning to the end.
  3. Filming with multiple cameras, as necessary, will be effective.
  4. When lighting is to be used, this must be discussed thoroughly with the successor. When it is to be used, care should be taken so as not to detract from the atmosphere of the site.
  5. Ways should be devised to record appropriate audio segments that are suited to the visuals.

- Method of editing

  1. A succession of tersely edited cuts or extreme changes in the angles may impair overall understanding of events and performing arts. Stable composition should be maintained.
  2. Since sounds and human voices from the location site are in themselves precious records, they should be utilized along with the visuals. Background music and sound effects should be used with adequate caution.

3. The use of narration, captions, titles, illustrations, etc. to aid understanding requires adequate caution.

8.7.4.3 Production and Filming Staff and Shooting and Editing Equipment

(1) Production staff

- Producer
- Production manager
- Director
- Assistant Director
- Researcher

(2) Filming staff

- Camera operator
- Assistant camera operator
- Audio
- Lighting
- Video engineer (VE)

(3) Editing staff

- Editor, editing operator
- Audio technician

– In the case of visual documentation for publicity/dissemination purposes, sound effects technicians and narrators will also become necessary.

- Shooting/editing equipment.

8.7.4.4 The Process from Editing to Delivery

8.7.5 Conservation and Utilization of Documentation

8.7.5.1 Raising Awareness of Conservation and Utilization

- Visual documentation for record retention
- Rentals to researchers, successors, and aficionados; as the visual image portion of local histories; as visual materials of cultural property survey reports; as academic materials to be held in museums and libraries
- Visual documentation for transmission/successor training
- Providing materials to successors (for use in practices and rehearsals); to be used in folklore facilities; as teaching materials for on-site classes as part of integrated study courses at schools; rentals to folk dance groups; as materials for tradition revival movements, etc.

- Visual documentation for publicity/dissemination
- For PR videos, including introductions to cultural properties/regional revival PR, etc.; as materials for lifelong learning/integrated learning programmes; as visual display materials at museums and resource centres; publication on the Internet, etc.

8.7.5.2 The Essential Element for Retention and Management and Utilization

- The digitization of information concerning the works and information management

    1. Title
    2. Subject of the documentation
    3. (Name of the recorded cultural property)
    4. Type of documentation and the media used
    5. Recording time
    6. Contents
    7. (Summary of the work in writing)
    8. Date of completion
    9. Filming period
    10. Outsourcer (organization responsible for the project, issuer)
    11. Contractor (person/organization responsible for the production)
    12. Performing organization (name of the preservation group, etc.)
    13. Place where documentation is stored (name, contact number)
    14. Mode of utilization (terms of use, contact number)

- Preparation of an easily viewed format
- Storage at an appropriate institution
- Monitoring and handover of storage location/terms of use, etc.
- Familiarizing of the related parties/related organizations
- Flexible responses to mutual use.

8.7.5.3 The Necessity for Archives

8.7.5.4 Consideration for Copyright and Related Rights

- Author's property rights
- Author's moral rights
- Neighbouring rights (performers' rights)
- The Agency for Cultural Affairs copyright web page
- Copyright Research and Information Centre.

8.7.5.5 For a Management that Looks Toward the Future

- Secondary use and the creation of secondary works
- Management of unedited materials.

8.8 Conclusion

In the past, before the advent of modern technology, intangible cultural heritage could not easily be revived when it failed to be handed down. Now, with advanced recording technology, it can be revived when sufficient written and/or visual documentation has been kept on a regular basis, even when the handing-down process has been interrupted. In the world of computers, the system defines a *recovery point* (RP) automatically, and recovers and revives the system exactly at that point. The documentation of intangible cultural heritage and its conservation, management and disclosure has significant importance as it can provide a 'recovery point' for future generations in case the heritage is not handed down.

Chapter 9
Anthropology of Intangible Cultural Heritage and Migration: An Uncharted Field

Cristina Amescua

Intangible Cultural Heritage (UNESCO 2003a) is a complex concept that has given rise to almost a decade of strong debates and profound reflection. In the last few years, it has been gaining a wider acceptance not only in the academic field, but also at the community level, with the growing participation of local practitioners and stakeholders, as well as NGOs and *community-based organizations* (CBOs). Anthropologists and other social scientists from all around the world were a fundamental force in its definition, mainly because ICH includes phenomena that have been traditionally addressed by anthropological research but that are now acquiring new meanings, or are being examined from innovative perspectives.

Current research into ICH has been growing in quantity, but it has also become more diverse in its topics: publications from the past ten years address several key aspects of the 2003 Convention (Kurin 2007; Schmitt 2008; Van Zanten 2004), as well as theoretical issues (Arizpe 2004; Baillie and Chippindale 2006; Bortolotto 2007; Cameron and Kenderdine 2007; Kirshenblatt-Gimblett 2004; Lenzerini 2011; Smith and Akagawa 2009; Tan et al. 2009). Problematic contemporary issues, such as ownership, copyright, and intellectual property (George 2010; Wendland 2004), or the use of virtual technologies in ICH (Cameron and Kenderdine 2007; Carrozzino et al. 2011; Langlais 2001; Yang et al. 2006) are being discussed, and the results of specific case studies are already being published (Arizpe 2011, 2009; Arizpe et al. 2011; Kato 2007; Zhu et al. 2011).

The first section of this chapter will discuss some aspects of the difference between tangible and intangible cultural heritage that I consider relevant for grounding any research into cultural heritage, particularly into intangible cultural

This chapter was written as part of the research project 'Culture and Migration: Intangible Cultural Heritage in the Contact Zones', supported with funding from PAPIIT IB 400212-2 (Universidad Nacional Autónoma de México).

C. Amescua (✉)
Centro Regional de Investigaciones Multidisciplinarias (UNAM), Av Universidad s/n Circuito II, Campus UAEM, Col. Chamilpa 62210 Cuernavaca, MOR, Mexico
e-mail: cristina.amescua@correo.crim.unam.mx

heritage. I will then present a field of study that has been relatively overlooked
when thinking about contemporary phenomena: the links between culture and
migration.

9.1 Cultural Heritage Dichotomies

At first glance, cultural heritage seems to be clearly split in two: tangible and
intangible heritage. UNESCO's (1972) *Convention Concerning the Protection of
the World Cultural and Natural Heritage* defines what was then considered as
'cultural heritage' as

> *monuments:* architectural works, works of monumental sculpture and painting, elements or
> structures of an archaeological nature, inscriptions, cave dwellings and combinations of
> features, which are of outstanding universal value from the point of view of history, art or
> science;
> *groups of buildings:* groups of separate or connected buildings which, because of their
> architecture, their homogeneity or their place in the landscape, are of outstanding universal
> value from the point of view of history, art or science;
> *sites:* works of man or the combined works of nature and man, and areas including
> archaeological sites which are of outstanding universal value from the historical, aesthetic,
> ethnological or anthropological point of view (UNESCO 1972).

Almost three decades later, after an intense international debate (that can be
traced through the works of Aikawa 2004; Arizpe 2006; Duvelle 2011), a fundamental void in this 1972 Convention was remedied with the adoption of the
Convention for the Safeguarding of the Intangible Cultural Heritage (2003a), thus
recognizing the importance of human creations that cannot be seen in a material
and durable form. This new Convention states that

> intangible cultural heritage means the practices, representations, expressions, knowledge,
> skills—as well as the instruments, objects, artefacts and cultural spaces associated
> therewith—that communities, groups and, in some cases, individuals recognize as part of
> their cultural heritage. This intangible cultural heritage, transmitted from generation to
> generation, is constantly recreated by communities and groups in response to their envi-
> ronment, their interaction with nature and their history, and provides them with a sense of
> identity and continuity, thus promoting respect for cultural diversity and human creativity.
> For the purposes of this Convention, consideration will be given solely to such intangible
> cultural heritage as is compatible with existing international human rights instruments, as
> well as with the requirements of mutual respect among communities, groups and indi-
> viduals, and of sustainable development (UNESCO 2003b).

At the core of this distinction, the materiality/immateriality dichotomy seems to
be the key defining element; but I want to argue against this idea. Of course, as all
the scholars devoted to the analysis of cultural heritage know, monuments,
buildings and sites have an intangible dimension that refers, for instance, to the
knowledge and beliefs behind their construction. On the other hand, intangible
heritage always has a material expression. Tangible and intangible cannot be
clearly distinguished. Nevertheless, there seems to be a common agreement that

the relevance of one or the other is what allows the analytical distinction as well as the classification of heritage as mainly tangible or intangible.

What I want to argue is that the key dichotomy in understanding both types of heritage is not materiality/immateriality, but rather staticity and dynamism. Indeed, tangible heritage refers to material products of human creativity that once created endure little or no transformation. They can be used, admired, resignified, preserved or protected for the use and joy of present and future generations. They are tokens of their specific socio-historical contexts that remain untouched (at least ideally) as witnesses of the times that precede us, and therefore include us, but that are no more. In contrast, intangible cultural heritage is dynamic and constantly moving; it is alive today, as it was several generations before. What keeps it going, passing down from one generation to the next, is its ability to transform itself, to be adapted by its practitioners and holders according to changing circumstances, and to adopt new elements and new meanings as its bearers endure movement and change.

Since anthropology is a discipline that has developed theories and methods for the study of cultural practices in live contexts, it is very well placed to analyse key issues such as the role of ICH in building and maintaining social bonds, change and continuity in ICH, transmission and interruption processes within ICH, and many others. In the next section, I will discuss the possibilities for the development of the anthropology of ICH in the context of mobility and migrations. I will then offer several examples of the paradoxical impact of migrations on intangible cultural heritage. Finally, I will present a case drawn from fieldwork that constitutes a first approach to several important issues that arise when analysing ICH in contact zones.

9.2 Intangible Cultural Heritage, Anthropology and Migration

The main characteristic of intangible cultural heritage is movement, transformation. Since groups of human beings are the repository of the knowledge and practices that constitute ICH, adaptation and dynamic change are the key elements that ensure the endurance of deeply grounded meanings that give a sense to collective life. For instance, in order to survive as a social and cultural practice, connecting live individuals and communities with their dead ancestors, and thus with their history (both personal and collective) and origins, as well as with their sense of belonging, new elements such as unused plastic plates and cups, colour photographs, or even Christmas lights have been adopted in the offerings of the Day of the Dead throughout the years. What has been altered is the form, not the meaning.

But movement is present not only in intangible cultural heritage, but also in its bearers. The communities that create and re-create it are themselves increasingly involved in mobility processes. Even though human migration is not a new phenomenon, in its current form it has grown both in diversity and in intensity. It is clear that more and more local communities are becoming sending or receiving places (or in some cases both) for migrants. But diversification can also be seen in their socio-demographic composition and in the growing variability of migratory experiences. The current intensity of migration is crystal clear when we consider that, according to the International Organization for Migration, 214 million people, or 3.1 % of today's total world population, is made up of migrants.

The relationship between culture and migration is very complex and relatively unexplored. Levitt (2005) points out that literature on migration normally overlooks its cultural dimensions. Indeed, the better part of migration studies are devoted to the quantification of the phenomenon, making substantial contributions regarding its characterization, its composition, the dynamics of immigration flows, its economic impacts and other issues of great interest; but the number of studies aimed at systematically exploring the impact of mobility on culture is considerably smaller.

A review of literature on migration and culture in the Americas (Arizpe et al. 2007) showed that research into the migration of Mexicans to the United States addresses topics as diverse as gender relations (Bettie 2003; Delgado Wise 2004; González-López 2005), changes in family structures (Cabrera Díaz and María del Carmen 2004; Hirsch 2003; Kanaiaupuni 2000), domestic violence (Chiarotti 2003; Fregoso 2003; Huacuz Elías and Barragán Solís 2003), social relations (Ho 1999), social and cultural reproduction (López-Castro 2003), and the circular movement of traditions (Ochoa-Serrano 2001; Sandoval Forero 1993). Anthropology and cultural studies have also provided an interesting analysis of cultural goods, including the iconography of migrants (Durand and Arias 2000), artistic productions resulting from the encounter of cultures (Griffith 2000; Maciel and Herrera-Sobek 1998; Vélez Ibañez 1999), identity transformations and reconfigurations (Anguiano Téllez and Hernández Madrid 2002; Deverell 2004; Valenzuela Arce 2004), and social and cultural agents in the immigration process (Mummert 1999; Velasco Ortiz 2002). Studies from these perspectives discuss issues such as membership, loyalty, cultural recomposition and ethnic self-adscription. In this review, we found works that recount the history of the formation of migrant neighbourhoods in various US cities, the organization of the Chicano movement, and the ensuing cultural expressions of Mexicans and Chicanos. All these issues are relevant because they account for the formation of bicultural communities resulting from long-term migration patterns.

It is evident that research addressing migration and culture is actually engaging with a wide variety of subjects. Indeed, "Culture is probably the broadest concept of all those used in the historical social sciences. It embraces a very large range of connotations, and thereby it is the cause perhaps of the most difficulty" (Wallerstein 1990). Nevertheless,

> research into the cultural dimensions of migrations in the era of globalization is one of the most fertile and innovative areas in contemporary anthropology and sociology. It is one of the great streams that feed the general reflection on global networks, new technologies of information and communication, dissemination of cultural industries, the transformation of identities, the production of hybrid cultures... But most of these studies deal with

migration and its collateral phenomena, rather than with the experience of migrants themselves (Le Bot 2011: 275–276).[1]

Now, a review of the literature devoted specifically to intangible cultural heritage in migratory contexts shows a substantially smaller critical mass. A decade after the adoption of the Convention, this topic is just beginning to be addressed by half a dozen authors (Amescua 2010a; Le Bot 2011; Gößwald 2007; Littlefield Kasfir 2004; Machuca 2011; Margolies 2011; Nettleford 2004; Vlachaki 2007).

However, many questions and problems arise when combining these two dimensions in a single field of study. One of the first questions might be: what about the intangible heritage of transnational communities? Does it remain in force only in communities of origin, or is it reproduced in receiving localities? What are the changes occurring at both ends? How are these changes being shaped, by which actors, and in which particular contexts and situations? Is intangible cultural heritage being lost as the process of assimilation of the second, third and fourth generations is consolidated? Does it affect the cultural practices of the receiving localities? In addition, considering that ICH is a key element in the generation of a sense of identity, belonging, and continuity, in creating links within cultural groups, as well as social ties, what about migrants who settle in new reception areas where there are still no transnational communities established? What is the personal and social impact of the lack of collective cultural activities that guide and give meaning to life?

9.3 Paradoxical Impacts of Migration on ICH

The complex relationship between the creation and re-creation of intangible cultural heritage in contexts of intense migration can be shown from a rapid analysis of a paradoxical reality. If the question is how migration affects the intangible cultural heritage of different communities across the planet, part of the answer lies in the fact that migration undermines the processes of transmission and continuity, but the other part shows that migration is a key element in maintaining and sustaining ICH manifestations and practices (Fig. 9.1).

The negative role of migration in ICH reproduction has been pointed out by some of the few authors who have written on the subject. Thus,

> the preservation and continuity of the cultural heritage of the people is facing challenges of various kinds. One of them is the result of migration processes which have increased in recent decades as an expression of globalization. Some see this phenomenon as the cause of the dissolution of the bonds that enable the transmission of knowledge and the transition between generations that accounts for the cultural continuity of a group. The result is then the abandonment of traditions and skills (some ancient) which have for a long time endured deep transformations and social upheavals (Machuca 2011: 281).[2]

---

[1] The author's translation.

[2] The author's translation.

Fig. 9.1 Day of the dead celebration, Georgia, USA (2009). *Source* Photo by Cristina Amescua

These negative effects are recognized in some of the candidature files of the elements that are currently inscribed in the Representative List of the Intangible Heritage of Humanity.[3]

---

[3] On November 1998, UNESCO's Executive Council at its 155th meeting adopted the *Guidelines for the Proclamation of the Masterpieces of Oral and Intangible Heritage of Humanity*. The Programme's objectives were "raising awareness of the importance of the oral and intangible heritage and the need to safeguard it; evaluating and listing the world's oral and intangible heritage; encouraging countries to establish national inventories and to take legal and administrative measures for the protection of their oral and intangible heritage; promoting the participation of traditional artists and local practitioners in identifying and revitalizing their Intangible Cultural Heritage." (UNESCO 2005f). UNESCO's member states were asked to present candidature files of items to be included in the List of Masterpieces through biannual proclamations which would cease to take place when the Convention came into effect. Thus three proclamations took place. In May 2001, 19 out of 32 candidatures presented were proclaimed; in November 2003, half of the 56 candidatures presented were proclaimed, and in November 2005, 43 of the 64 proposals were selected. When the Convention became effective in April, 2006, the 90 elements recorded in the Masterpieces list were incorporated into the Representative List of Intangible Heritage. At the Fourth Meeting of the Intergovernmental Committee for the Safeguarding of Intangible Cultural Heritage, held in Abu Dhabi, United Arab Emirates, in September 2009, 76 new elements were registered, and the List of Intangible Heritage in Need of Urgent Safeguarding was launched, with the registration of 12 elements.

The candidature file of the Cross Crafting Tradition in Lithuania and Latvia states that an "…unfavourable factor [for this traditional practice] is the constant decrease in the population of local communities. The older generation who cherished the tradition of cross-crafting is dying out. Forced by today's economic development, young people move to the cities" (UNESCO 2001). With regard to the Andean Cosmovision of the Kallawaya in Bolivia

> … young people in search of employment are forced to abandon their communities. This situation has an impact on development and transmission. The old priest-healers cannot hand down their knowledge and cosmovision because of the cruel lack of students. The Kallayawas communities are suffering a strong demographic transformation. In fact, during certain seasons, the ayllu is only inhabited by people of age and women who are in charge of ensuring the production of medicinal plants. This temporary dismemberment of the families tends to produce severe consequences within communities (…). Social structure is disrupted. Nowadays, Kallawaya communities are split into two groups: the Kallawaya living in the communities, and those living in the cities (UNESCO 2003c).[4]

The transmission of the musical and poetical genre known as Ahellil, emblematic of the Zenete population of Gourara in Algeria is endangered because "the lack of job opportunities at regional level has produced, during the last 20 years, a massive immigration of the Gouraris to the northern cities of Algeria. Mature men, exactly those who master Ahelli, are frequently absent from their communities, and so are unable to transmit a minimum of their knowledge" (UNESCO 2005a).[5]

Two of the elements Zambia has inscribed in the Representative List present immigration as a threat to the continuity of such traditions. On the one hand, in the case of the Makishi Masquerade, "the growth of urban towns in Zambia and the demand for wage labour has attracted many young men to the towns. There are many young members from the Makishi practising communities who are migrating to the cities, thereby abandoning their rich tradition" (UNESCO 2005b). On the other hand, the Gule Wamkulu, a multinational element, inscribed by Malawi, Mozambique and Zambia, is threatened by the loss of the young population, in ways more tragic than emigration: "Rural to urban migration, especially of the younger and active generation in search of jobs and the death of young and productive people due to HIV/AIDS, will affect the Gule Wamkulu performances, which require physical fitness" (UNESCO 2005c).

So far, we have presented examples of the negative impacts of people leaving their homelands (emigration), but in the candidature files we can also find arguments presenting immigration as a menace to traditional practices: "Industrial development stimulated the mass influx of migrants—representatives of other cultures, ethnoses, and nations changed the proportion of residents and newcomers in favour of the latter, forcing intensive russification on the indigenous population" (UNESCO 2005d).

---

[4] The author's translation from French.
[5] The author's translation from French.

However, it is also necessary to acknowledge a totally different side of the equation. For instance, the candidature file of the Day of the Dead presented by Mexico states that 'Indigenous migrants to the United States and Canada return each year to their villages to celebrate remember and coexist with their ancestors and family during the so-called Day of the Dead (...)" (UNESCO 2005e). Similarly, during field work it is common to find multiple examples of how migration has been an important factor in ensuring the survival of various cultural events locally. Thus, in Zacualpan de Amilpas, Morelos, funding for the town's main festivity dedicated to Santa Catarina comes largely from migrants who are in the United States. Through this distant participation, those who are not physically there affirm the continuity of their belonging to their community of origin, as their names, along with the towns to which they migrated, and the amount of money provided, are outlined on a large bulletin board set out on one side of the church. Their names are repeated through the loudspeakers surrounding the main square, as the animator of the dances mentions one by one those who helped to make the celebration possible.

Temacapulín, a small town located in the highlands of Jalisco, which throughout the year is inhabited only by about forty families, comes to life when hundreds of 'missing children' (*hijos ausentes*) come back in December and January to celebrate the Virgen de los Remedios, the patron saint of the town. In addition to religious celebrations, including masses and 'mañanitas' for the Virgin, during the eight days of the celebration meals are offered to all people and dances enlivened by various musical groups are organized. Each day is sponsored by a group of 'missing children': the first day it is Temacapulín's yearly inhabitants who are in charge; the next the missing children from León, Guanajuato; the third day it is the turn of the missing children from Mexico City, then those of Guadalajara, and finally, the missing children from the US are in charge of the last day of the celebration. Each of these groups works hard on their day's preparations, seeking to outdo each other. And so the feast of the Virgin is the framework within which the natives of Temacapulín, both those who have remained and those who have left, as well as those who were not born there but recognize it as their place of symbolic origin, communicate, update, recognize and get to know each other, creating ties that give them identity and a sense of belonging. The children of the 'missing children' meet and start friendships that will later continue through the social networks on electronic media. The return of migrants to Temacapulín, organized around the religious holiday, goes far beyond this. From dawn, small groups of people take the opportunity to climb the hill of the Cross, to go fishing in the river or visit the canyon, to bathe in the hot springs or visit the chapel of Cristo de La Peñita. Thus, migrants reappropriate the ancient landscape, walking the same paths as their grandparents and great-grandparents, hearing the stories of their parents when they were children and played in those same hills, and thus building their personal stories. Indeed, as Machuca puts it,

> the religious arena is still a fundamental articulation point. The festive cycles, rites and celebrations for the patron saints in the villages acquire a mnemothetic referential

importance on the temporal axis. Their cyclic character persists over the labour time imperative. Festivities in receiving localities, as well as the itineraries of those who return to the places or origin, are both oriented and synchronized with the events taking places in their homelands (2011: 285).[6]

9.4 Intangible Cultural Heritage in the Contact Zones: Some Initial Clues for a Deeper Understanding

The above examples illustrate both the negative and the positive effects deriving from the relationship between migration and intangible heritage in migrants' sending communities. But in order to fully comprehend the phenomena associated with migration processes it is necessary to go beyond the static and territorial conceptualization of culture and communities. In a world characterized by a global-scale economy, technological achievements that allow faster and less expensive transfers, satellite interconnections fostering global circulation of ideas, imaginaries and cultural contents through great innovations in the field of information and communications technology and through the circulation of immigrants who are constantly crossing national borders, it is almost impossible to think that communities and cultures are circumscribed by clearly delimited boundaries. This does not mean that the role of territories and national boundaries in the construction of everyday human experience should be overlooked: real and imagined borders do exist, and are there serving as markers of the 'in' and 'out', of what belongs or not. Borders are edges cutting though trajectories, establishing controls, determining routes, functioning as walls or opening gateways. This is something that migrations studies need to consider. Nevertheless "cultural creation flourishes in voids, margins, borders, in difficult (and frequently conflictive) encounters between different cultures, and even in the fractures within those cultures, in the contact zones and the interstices. Such creations are nourished by divergences, displacements, convulsions and ruptures, by the questioning of identities" (Le Bot 2006).[7]

Pratt defines contact zones as "social spaces where cultures meet, clash, and grapple with each other, often in contexts of highly asymmetrical relations of power, such as colonialism, slavery, or their aftermaths as they are lived out in many parts of the world today" (1991: 34). Borderland regions tend to be the characteristic contact zones, but diversification in points of origin and destination in the trajectories of migrants have been turning a great number of 'inland' areas into contact zones. This is exactly the case with the US South-east, an area I have been studying since 2006 and that until the 1980s had almost non-existent immigration rates, while between the 1990s and the year 2000 it experienced

---

[6] The author's translation from Spanish.

[7] The author's translation from Spanish.

State and position	Latino population 1990	Latino population 2000	State population (%)	Growth (%) 1990–2000
Georgia	108,922	435,227	5.3	299.6
North Carolina	76,726	378,963	4.7	393.9
Virginia	160,288	329,540	4.7	105.6
Tennessee	32,741	123,838	2.2	278.2
Louisiana	93,044	107,738	2.4	15.8
South Carolina	30,551	98,076	2.4	311.2
Arkansas	19,876	86,866	3.3	337.0
Alabama	24,629	75,830	1.7	207.9
Kentucky	21,984	59,939	1.5	172.6
Mississippi	15,931	39,569	1.4	148.4
West Virginia	8,489	12,279	0.7	44.6

Fig. 9.2 Latino population in the US south-east, 1990–2000. *Source* US Census Bureau, 2000

exponential growth in the Latino population, ranging from 44.6 to 393.9 %, as shown in the Fig. 9.2.

This region is particularly interesting for current studies of migration and culture, since the relative novelty of this social phenomenon allows researchers to track and analyse cultural changes as they occur. The research I've been conducting could be categorized as a multilocal 'patchwork ethnography' (Lowenhaupt Tsing 2005), because fieldwork comprised several sending communities in Morelos, México and several receiving suburban sites within the Atlanta Metropolitan Area in the US (the latter are the ones that I am considering as contact zones). I have been focusing mainly on cross-cultural perceptions between Mexican immigrants and American citizens regarding each other and their cultures. But I have also analysed several cultural practices that can be understood as intangible cultural heritage where a space of conviviality among cultures is emerging (Amescua 2006, 2011, 2012).

I present here a brief example drawn from my fieldwork that will allow me to illustrate several of the issues that need further research when engaging with the subject of migration and intangible cultural heritage.

The Dragon Boat[8] festival is a traditional event in several cities of East and South East Asia (including China, Taiwan, Hong Kong, Korea, and Macao), whose legendary origins can be traced back to 278 BCE. This practice, both in its traditional form (associated with religious ceremonies and folk festivals) and as a modern sport, is very much alive not only in Asia but also in countries such as the US, Canada, the Netherlands, the United Kingdom, Spain, Australia, and the Philippines.

In 2009 and 2010, the Archdiocese of Atlanta Young Adult Ministry organized a Multicultural Dragon Boat Festival for its parishioners, inviting them to

---

[8] A Dragon Boat is a long human-powered wooden boat built in various designs and sizes and painted in bright colours. Traditional boats have a dragon head built in their bow. The crew is typically made up of twenty paddlers sitting in pairs facing towards the bow of the boat, one drummer or caller facing the paddlers, and one steerer at the rear of the boat.

Fig. 9.3 Dragon boat festival, Georgia, USA (2009). *Source* Photo by Cristina Amescua

'celebrate a fun afternoon of teamwork and camaraderie while we celebrate our diversity'.[9]

On Sunday 16 May 2010, I conducted participant observation during the festival. After registration, participants were given bracelets of different colours (blue, green, orange, and yellow), each one representing a team. This was a way of ensuring that people attending together were not paired in the same team.

The participants in the celebration were indeed from several ethnic origins including White Americans, African Americans, Latinos and Asians. The programme started with an open-air mass, followed by a light lunch. During those two moments I observed that peopled tended to group together according to their respective ethnic origins (and of course according to their previous acquaintance). There was no substantial communication going on (Fig. 9.3).

When the organizers signalled the beginning of the race, participants had to group according to their bracelet colour and a trainer would begin to explain to each group how the paddling was supposed to be done.

I was a member of the blue group along with six white Americans, five African Americans, one Asian and seven Latinos. Most of us had never participated in a dragon boat race, although one of the white Americans was an expert paddler. As the trainer gave instructions in English I noticed some discomfort growing among

---

[9] The author's translation of the original flyer in Spanish.

my group. The Latinos took two or three steps back as if they were thinking of running away. The English speakers, particularly the expert paddler, were giving each other puzzled looks. A tense and uncomfortable silence grew up around the trainer's voice. At one point I started to wonder if the Latinos could understand anything of what the trainer was saying. I was afraid of asking since I felt they might feel offended by my assuming they could not speak English. But when I turned around and saw that the other teams were already picking their team names, cheering, and heading towards the water, I overcame my fear, and asked if they wanted me to translate. They nodded in silent agreement. Everyone was having trouble verbalizing what we were all thinking: 'How on earth are we going to complete a task that requires teamwork, when we cannot even understand each other?' Finally, we managed to complete the verbal training and got into our boat.

All the other boats were already ahead in the river, while we kept on trying to move ours. The first few paddles were a total disaster. We kept knocking into each other, while bringing copious amounts of water into the boat and not moving an inch. The silence among us grew thicker. Our trainer, serving now as the boat's steerer, went on with his instructions, while I kept translating over the rhythmic sound of the drum. Slowly the boat began to move away from the dock. We were getting better at working together, our movements gained in coordination and synchronicity with every beat of the drum, which is considered to be the heartbeat of the dragon boat. As we moved down the river, the ambience began to become more relaxed. Jokes and cheers both in Spanish and in English were replacing the uncomfortable silence that had prevailed moments before. Making constant efforts not to bang on my seat partner I went on with my self-assumed translator role, until one of the Latino team fellows said in a loud voice, "No, he (the trainer) did not say that; he said we need to bend down some more". Well, I thought with half a smile, he does speak English after all. And from then on, I kept my mouth shut, and concentrated on overcoming my natural clumsiness with physical tasks.

After one hour of training, all teams took a break to relax and drink some water. Salsa music was coming out of the loudspeakers, and several couples started a spontaneous dance contest. Not only the Latinos were polishing the improvised dance floor, some of the Anglos and a couple of African Americans also jumped in. People had begun to mingle. After a while the organizers signalled the beginning of the race. Each team headed with more confidence into their boats as we all rowed to the middle of the river. Our trainer explained that we would race four consecutive times and the last boat to reach the finishing line would be eliminated. The winner would be the first team to cross the line during the fourth race.

The first race started, and our team was not eliminated. Then the second came, with us still in the game. Our instructor kept telling us to follow the beat, to concentrate on our coordination without paying attention to the other competitors. The third race ended and we were still on. With each race, a team spirit began building up in our boat. We were all laughing and having a great time; we were smiling at each other. There were no more averting gazes, no more uncomfortable silences, no more side glances. Instead, we were cheering and uttering encouraging words: "we did it, we're still in the race!" said a blond teenager, "ora sí compas, a echarle todos los kilos, esta es la buena",[10] replied the eldest of the Latinos, whom I later learned came from Guatemala.

The fourth race began, and only the sound of the drum could be heard along with the trainer's voice repeating "go, go, go, go". We crossed the finish line and we all turned round to look at the other team. We could not make out who had won. After a long pause, the verdict came from the loudspeakers: "the blue team wins the race!" That was us! We could not believe it. A burst of laughter followed our unbelieving gazes, pride and satisfaction had replaced all discomfort. While we were paddling towards the dock, everyone began to comment: "this was so much fun" said the blonde teenager's boyfriend, "Yo pensé que esto iba a ser un desastre, y mira lo que logramos",[11] my seat partner told me, "I can't believe we did it!" added the expert paddler with a huge smile. The Asian guy who was sitting in the last row didn't say a thing, but his shy grin had turned into a wide and happy laugh.

I see this experience as a point of entry to identify some of the relevant questions that arise from the analysis of multicultural contact through ICH. In this case, the Dragon Boat festival was the framework within which cultural interactions occurred. A more in-depth analysis should consider questions such as: were participants aware of the ancestral and cultural dimensions involved in he festival? Was this knowledge, or the lack of it, important in their decision to participate and in the appreciation of the practice itself? How did participation in this cultural activity, that entailed elements such as teamwork and actual physical collaboration (as opposed to rhetorical or theoretical collaboration), change the mutual perceptions of each other for participants of different ethnic origins? The outcomes of this experience, at least the ones I could observe,[12] were clearly positive. The general ambience changed considerably from tension and awkwardness to a joint sentiment of fulfilment and joy. If this could be achieved with only several hours of intercultural interaction, what could happen if spaces of conviviality within contact zones were to be built around practices and manifestations that constitute ICH for the different cultures coexisting in a single space?

9.5 Final Comments

Interactions between intangible cultural heritage and migration constitute an issue that needs to be addressed from a wide variety of perspectives. ICH can illustrate the complex interactions between global forces and local realities (something I have not explored in this chapter).

---

[10] "This is it bros, let's give it everything we have. This is our last chance."

[11] "I thought this was going to be a disaster, and look what we just did."

[12] It is important to make clear that I was not able to conduct in-depth interviews, since I encountered this event while doing fieldwork for a research project that had other aims and objectives. I am using it here just to give an example of the need for systematic research into the relationship between ICH and migration.

When analysing the impacts of migration on intangible cultural heritage, point of view is critical: what happens in sending areas is not the same as what happens in receiving localities.

On the other hand, in considering one or several of the issues discussed in this chapter, it is theoretically and methodologically relevant to be constantly aware of a fundamental distinction within intangible cultural heritage. This distinction could be conceptualized in several ways. At the more basic level it is what I called at the beginning of this text the immaterial and the material dimensions present in both tangible and intangible heritage. But in order to be more precise, I find it useful to elaborate a little more.

In the case of intangible cultural heritage, when we speak of a cultural practice, of a representation (in its theatrical sense), or of particular techniques (for example those involved in traditional craftsmanship), we are in fact talking about the expressive dimension of ICH, the one that can be seen. On the other hand, when we refer to the knowledge, the cosmogonies and cosmologies, or even to other elements included in the Convention's definition, such as intergenerational transmission or the 'sense of identity and continuity', we are speaking of the reflexive, abstract or symbolic dimension of ICH.

Defining which of these two dimensions we want the research to focus on will determine the theoretical and methodological choices that are to be made. When addressing the expressive dimension of ICH, traditional ethnographic methods and techniques are an ideal tool for gathering the required data, while when focusing on the expressive or symbolic dimension of ICH, tools such as discourse and narrative analysis will be more in order to convey all the meanings and symbols that are transmitted and created in the minds of practitioners and stakeholders. Finally, I think that symbolic and cognitive anthropology can be very fruitful theoretical frameworks for understanding this latter dimension, while more traditional anthropological theories might help to better understand the expressive dimension.

References

Aikawa, Noriko, 2004: "An Historical Overview of the Preparation of the UNESCO International Convention for the Safeguarding of the Intangible Cultural Heritage", in: *Museum International*, 56: 137–49. doi: 10.1111/j.1350-0775.2004.00468.x.

Amescua, Cristina, 2006: "La emergencia de nuevas formas de transnacionalidad en la nueva era de las migraciones entre México y Estados Unidos: el caso Amilcingo y Norcross" (MBA Thesis, Universidad Nacional Autónoma de México, Mexico City).

Amescua, Cristina, 2010a: Cultura y migración. El patrimonio cultural inmaterial en las zonas de contacto: ¿una lucha por la autenticidad o una opción para la convivencia? *Cuadernos de Migración Internacional* 6. (Mexico City: Universidad Iberoamericana).

Amescua, Cristina, 2011: "Percepciones sobre los migrantes mexicanos en el condado de Gwinnett, Georgia: fricciones y encuentros en el sur estadounidense" (Norteamérica, Mexico City: Centro de Investigaciones sobre América del Norte—UNAM).

Amescua, Cristina, 2012: "Percepciones sobre las culturas en las zonas de contacto: fricciones y encuentros en el caso de la migración mexicana al sur de Estados Unidos" (Doctoral Thesis, Mexico: Universidad Nacional Autónoma de México).

Anguiano Téllez, María Eugenia; Hernández Madrid, Miguel J., 2002: *Migración internacional e identidades cambiantes* (Mexico City: El Colegio de Michoacán; El Colegio de la Frontera Norte).

Arizpe, Lourdes, 2004: "Intangible Cultural Heritage, Diversity and Coherence", in: *Museum International*, 56: 130–36. doi: 10.1111/j.1350-0775.2004.00467.x.

Arizpe, Lourdes, 2006: "Los debates internacionales en torno al patrimonio cultural inmaterial", in: *Cuicuilco*, 13: 13–27.

Arizpe, Lourdes, 2009: *El Patrimonio Cultural Inmaterial de México: Ritos y Festividades en Morelos*, 1st ed (Mexico City: Miguel Ángel Porrúa, CRIM–UNAM, CONACULTA, Cámara de Diputados).

Arizpe, Lourdes, 2011: *Compartir el Patrimonio Cultural Inmaterial: Narrativas y Representaciones* (Mexico City: CRIM-UNAM, CONACULTA–DGCP).

Arizpe, Lourdes; Amescua, Cristina; Luque, José Carlos, 2007: *Migración y Cultura en América Latina y el Caribe: Bibliografía Seleccionada* (Mexico City: Centro Regional de Investigaciones Multidisciplinarias).

Arizpe, Lourdes; Amescua, Cristina; Pérez, Edith, et al. 2011: *El Patrimonio Cultural Cívico: la Memoria Política como Capital Social* (Mexico City: Miguel Ángel Porrúa, Cámara de Diputados).

Baillie, Britt; Chippindale, Christopher, 2006: "Tangible–Intangible Cultural Heritage: A Sustainable Dichotomy?" Paper for the 7th Annual Cambridge Heritage Seminar, McDonald Institute for Archaeological Research, University of Cambridge, UK, Cambridge, 13 May. *Conservation and Management of Archaeological Sites*, 8: 174–76. doi: 10.1179/175355206x265814.

Bettie, Julie, 2003: *Women Without Class: Girls, Race, and Identity* (Berkeley, Los Angeles: The University of California Press).

Bortolotto, Chiara, 2007: "From Objects to Processes: UNESCO's 'Intangible Cultural Heritage'", in: *Journal of Museum Ethnography*, 19: 21–33.

Cabrera Díaz, Carmen María del, 2004: *Influencia de la migración internacional, México–Estados Unidos, en el calendario de la nupcialidad* (México: El Colegio de México).

Cameron, Fiona; Kenderdine, Sarah, 2007: *Theorizing Digital Cultural Heritage: A Critical Discourse* (Washington, DC, Smithsonian Center for Folklife and Cultural Heritage) 59: 465.

Carrozzino, Marcello; Scucces, Alessandra; Leonardi, Rosario, et al. 2011: "Virtually Preserving the Intangible Heritage of Artistic Handicraft", in: *Journal of Cultural Heritage*, 12: 82–87. doi: 10.1016/j.culher.2010.10.002.

Chiarotti, Susana, 2003: *La trata de mujeres: sus conexiones y desconexiones con la migración y los derechos humanos* (antiago de Chile: CELADE/CEPAL/BID (Población y Desarrollo/39)): 39: 33.

Delgado Wise, Raúl, 2004: *Nuevas tendencias y desafíos de la migración internacional México–Estados Unidos* (Mexico City: Miguel Angel Porrúa).

Deverell, William, 2004: *Whitewashed adobe. The Rise of Los Angeles and the Remaking of Its Mexican Past* (Berkeley, Los Angeles: The University of California Press).

Durand, Jorge; Arias, Patricia, 2000: *La experiencia migrante: iconografía de la migración México–Estados Unidos* (Tlaquepaque: Instituto Tecnológico de Estudios Superiores de Occidente).

Duvelle, Cécile, 2011: "Los instrumentos Normativos Internacionales de la UNESCO sobre la cultura: una mirada al pasado, una mirada al futuro", in: Arizpe, L. (Ed.): *Compartir el Patrimonio Cultural Inmaterial: Narrativas y Representaciones* (Mexico City: Centro Regional de Investigaciones Multidisciplinarias UNAM, Dirección General de Culturas Populares/CONACULTA): 15–24.

Fregoso, Rosa L., 2003: *meXicana Encounters: The Making of Social Identities on the Borderlands* (Berkeley, Los Angeles: University of California Press).

118   C. Amescua

George, E. Wanda, 2010: "Intangible Cultural Heritage, in: Ownership, Copyrights, and Tourism", in: *International Journal of Culture Tourism and Hospitality Research*, 4: 376–88.

González-López, Gloria, 2005: *Erotic Journeys. Mexican Immigrants and Their Sex Lives* (Berkeley, Los Angeles: The University of California Press).

Gößwald, Udo, 2007: "Born in Europe: An International Programme on Representing Migrant Experiences in European Museums", in: *International Journal of Intangible Heritage*, 2: 138–44.

Griffith, James, 2000: *Hecho a Mano: The Traditional Arts of Tucson's Mexican American Community* (Tucson: The University of Arizona Press).

Hirsch, Jennifer S., 2003: *A Courtship After Marriage: Sexuality and Love in Mexican Transnational Families* (Berkeley, Los Angeles: The University of California Press).

Ho, Christine, 1999: "Caribbean Transnationalism as a Gendered Process", in: *Latin American Perpectives*, 6: 34–54.

Huacuz Elías, MG; Barragán Solís, A., 2003: *Diluyendo las fronteras: género, migración internacional y violencia conyugal en Guanajuato* (Guanajuato: Gobierno del Estado de Guanajuato, Instituto de la Mujer Guanajuatense).

Kanaiaupuni, SM, 2000: "Reframing the Migration Question: an Analysis of Men, Women, and Gender in Mexico", in: *Social Forces*, 78: 1311–47.

Kato, Kumi, 2007: "Prayers for the Whales: Spirituality and Ethics of a Former Whaling Community—Intangible Cultural Heritage for Sustainability", in: *International Journal of Cultural Property*, 14: 283–313. doi: 10.1017/S0940739107070191.

Kirshenblatt-Gimblett, Barbara, 2004: "Intangible Heritage as Metacultural Production". in: *Museum International*, 56: 52–65. doi: 10.1111/j.1350-0775.2004.00458.x.

Kurin, Richard, 2007: "Key Factors in Implementing the 2003 Convention on Safeguarding Intangible Cultural Heritage", in: *Intangible Heritage*, 9.

Langlais, Dominique, 2001: "Cybermuseology and Intangible Heritage", *Knowledge Creation Diffusion Utilization*, 7281. at: <http://www.yorku.ca/etopia/docs/conference/Langlais.pdf>.

Le Bot, Yvon, 2006: *Migraciones, Fronteras y Creaciones Culturales*. Foro Internacional vol 85 XLVI, issue 3 (Mexico City: El Colegio de México): 533–548.

Le Bot, Yvon, 2011: "Migrantes transnacionales y reconstrucciones culturales", in: Arizpe, Lourdes (Ed.) *Compartir el Patrimonio Cultural Inmaterial: Narrativas y Representaciones* (Mexico City: CRIM–UNAM, CONACULTA–DGCP): 273–280.

Lenzerini, F., 2011: "Intangible Cultural Heritage: The Living Culture of Peoples". in: *European Journal of International Law*, 22: 101–120. doi: 10.1093/ejil/chr006.

Levitt, Peggy, 2005: "Building Bridges: What Migration Scholarship and Cultural Sociology Have to Say to Each Other", in: *Poetics*, 3: 49–62.

Littlefield Kasfir, S.; Yai, Olabiyi Babalola Joseph, 2004: "Tema de debate actual: Autenticidad y diáspora", in: *Museum International*, 221–222: 190–197.

López-Castro, Gloria, 2003: *Diáspora michoacana* (Zamora: El Colegio de Michoacán; Gobierno del Estado de Michoacán).

Lowenhaupt Tsing, Anna, 2005: *Friction. An Ethnography of Global Connection* (Princeton, NJ: Princeton University Press).

Maciel, DR; Herrera-Sobek, M., 1998: *Culture Across Borders. Mexican Immigration and Popular Culture* (Tucson, Arizona: The University of Arizona Press).

Machuca, Antonio, 2011: "Transmisión y producción del sentido en el fenómeno migratorio: su incidencia en la conceptualización del Patrimonio Inmaterial", in: Arizpe, L., (Ed.) *Compartir el Patrimonio Cultural Inmaterial: Narrativas y Representaciones* (Mexico City: CRIM–UNAM, CONACULTA–DGCP): 281–310.

Margolies, Daniel S., 2011: "Music in the 21st century. Transmission of Texas-Mexican Conjunto Music in the 21st century", in: *International Journal of Intangible Heritage*, 6: 26–33.

Mummert, Gail, 1999: *Fronteras fragmentadas* (Zamora: El Colegio de Michoacán; Centro de Investigación y Desarrollo del Estado de Michoacán).

Nettleford, Rex, 2004: "Migration, Transmission and Maintenance of the Intangible Heritage", in: *Museum International*, 56: 78–83. doi: 10.1111/j.1350-0775.2004.00460.x.

Ochoa-Serrano, Á., 2001: *Y nos volvemos a encontrar: migración, identidad y tradición cultural* (Zamora: El Colegio de Michoacán; Centro de Investigación y Desarrollo del Estado de Michoacán).

Pratt, Mary Louise, 1991: "Arts of the Contact Zone", *Profession*, 91: 33–40. at: <http://writing.colostate.edu/files/classes/6500/File_EC147617-ADE5-3D9CC89FF0384AECA15B.pdf>.

Sandoval Forero, EA., 1993: *Migración e identidad: experiencias del exilio* (Toluca: Universidad Autónoma del Estado de México): 213.

Schmitt, Thomas M., 2008: "The UNESCO Concept of Safeguarding Intangible Cultural Heritage: Its Background and Marrakchi Roots", in: *International Journal of Heritage Studies*, 14: 95–111. doi: 10.1080/13527250701844019.

Smith, Laurajane; Akagawa, Natsuko, 2009: *Intangible Heritage* (Abingdon, UK: Routledge).

Tan, Guoxin; Hao, Tingley; Zhong, Zheng, 2009: "A Knowledge Modeling Framework for Intangible Cultural Heritage Based on Ontology", Paper for the 2nd International Symposium on Knowledge Acquisition and Modeling, KAM 09, Wuhan, China, 06 February. doi: 10.1109/KAM.2009.17:304–307.   at: http://ieeexplore.ieee.org/stamp/stamp.jsp?tp=&arnumber=5362170.

UNESCO 1972: *Convention Concerning the Protection of the World Cultural and Natural Heritage*. at: <http://whc.unesco.org/en/conventiontext/> (12 June 2011).

UNESCO 2001: *Candidature Files for the Proclamation of Oral and Intangible Heritage of Humanity—Cross Crafting Tradition—Lithuania and Latvia* (Printed files consulted at the Information Centre on Intangible Cultural Heritage, UNESCO, Paris, May–June 2007).

UNESCO 2003a: *Convention for the Safeguarding of the Intangible Cultural Heritage*. <http://www.unesco.org/culture/ich/index.php?lg=en&pg=00022> (12 June 2011).

UNESCO 2003b: *Convention for the Safeguarding of the Intangible Cultural Heritage*. <http://www.unesco.org/culture/ich/index.php?lg=en&pg=00022> (12 June 2011).

UNESCO 2003c: *Candidature Files for the Proclamation of Oral and Intangible Heritage of Humanity—the Andean Cosmovision of the Kallawaya—Bolivia* (Printed files consulted at the Information Centre on Intangible Cultural Heritage, UNESCO, Paris, May–June 2007).

UNESCO 2005a: *Candidature Files for the Proclamation of Oral and Intangible Heritage of Humanity—Ahellil of Gourara—Algeria* (Printed files consulted at the Information Centre on Intangible Cultural Heritage, UNESCO, Paris, May–June 2007).

UNESCO 2005b: *Candidature Files for the Proclamation of Oral and Intangible Heritage of Humanity—the Makishi Masquerade—Zambia* (Printed files consulted at the Information Centre on Intangible Cultural Heritage, UNESCO, Paris, May–June 2007).

UNESCO 2005c: *Candidature Files for the Proclamation of Oral and Intangible Heritage of Humanity—the Gule Wamkulu—Malawi, Mozambique, Zambia* (Printed files consulted at the Information Centre on Intangible Cultural Heritage, UNESCO, Paris, May–June 2007).

UNESCO 2005d: *Candidature Files for the Proclamation of Oral and Intangible Heritage of Humanity—Alonkho, Yakut Heroic Epos—Russian Federation* (Printed files consulted at the Information Centre on Intangible Cultural Heritage, UNESCO, Paris, May–June 2007).

UNESCO 2005e: *Candidature Files for the Proclamation of Oral and Intangible Heritage of Humanity—the Day of the Dead—Mexico* (Printed files consulted at the Information Centre on Intangible Cultural Heritage, UNESCO, Paris, May–June 2007).

UNESCO 2005f: *Proclamations of the Masterpieces of Oral and Intangible Heritage of Humanity* (Printed files consulted at the Information Centre on Intangible Cultural Heritage, UNESCO, Paris, May–June 2007).

Valenzuela Arce, José Manuel, 2004: *Renacerá la palabra. Identidades y diálogo intercultural* (Mexico City: El Colegio de la Frontera Norte).

Van Zanten, Wim, 2004: "Constructing New Terminology for Intangible Cultural Heritage", in: *Museum International*, 56: 36–44. doi: 10.1111/j.1350-0775.2004.00456.

Velasco Ortiz, Laura, 2002: *El regreso de la comunidad: migración indígena y agentes étnicos, los mixtecos en la frontera México Estados Unidos* (Mexico City: El Colegio de México, Centro de Estudios Sociológicos; El Colegio de la Frontera Norte).

Vélez Ibañez, C., 1999: Visiones de frontera. Las culturas mexicanas del sudoeste de Estados Unidos. Mexico City. Miguel Ángel Porrúa, Centro de Investigaciones y Estudios Superiores en Antropología Social (CIESAS).

Vlachaki, María, 2007: "An Educational Programme about Migration in Crossing Cultures through the Intangible Heritage: An Educational Programme about Migration in Greece", in: *International Journal of Intangible Heritage*, 2: 94–102.

Wallerstein, Immanuel, 1990: *Culture as the Ideological battleground of the Modern World-System. Global Culture: Nationalism, Globalization and Modernity* (London: SAGE Publications): 31–55.

Wendland, Wend, 2004: "Intangible Heritage and Intellectual Property: Challenges and Future Prospects", in: *Museum International*, 56: 97–107. doi: 10.1111/j.1350-0775.2004.00463.x.

Yang, Cheng; Peng, Dongmei; Sun, Shouqian, 2006: "Creating a Virtual Activity for the Intangible Culture Heritage", Paper for the 16th International Conference on Artificial Reality and Telexistence Workshops, ICAT06, Hangzhou, China. doi: 10.1109/ICAT.2006.52. <http://ieeexplore.ieee.org/stamp/stamp.jsp?tp=&arnumber=4089329> (06 February 2010).

Zhu, Bin; Huang, Long Xiang; Yang, Jin-Sheng, et al. 2011: "Analysis of the Nominations of Acupuncture and Moxibustion of Traditional Chinese Medicine for Inscription on the Representative List of the Intangible Cultural Heritage of Humanity", in: *Zhongguo zhen jiu Chinese acupuncture moxibustion*, 31: 193–197.

Annexe
General Discussion: Identifying Key Issues

The processes of 'heritagization' always entail the creation of regimes of quality control and evaluation. Anthropological knowledge along with its particular methodologies and techniques may help clarify issues such as the frequent incompatibility between the world views of the holders of intangible cultural heritage and forms of organization together with the requirements of governments, non-governmental organizations and activist movements, as well as the dynamics of power holders at different levels of the process of selection, inventorying and inscription.

In the last few years, the International Convention for the Safeguarding of Intangible Cultural Heritage has achieved worldwide recognition of the importance of intangible cultural heritage in international politics and development. However, a more concerted effort is now required in scientific research into intangible cultural heritage as the Convention deepens and expands its policy-driven actions. While the International Social Science Council and the International Union of Anthropological and Ethnological Sciences worked closely with UNESCO in the early stages in setting up the Convention, at the General Assembly of State Parties to the Convention in 2010 a renewed interest was expressed—and included in changes to the statutes—in collaborating with researchers. Accordingly, in December 2010 the Commission on Intangible Cultural Heritage was formally created in the International Social Science Council. Its aim is to strengthen the networks of researchers working on intangible cultural heritage and in relevant fields and to foster a new synergy in discussions on key issues concerning the Convention.

Given the increased interest in intangible cultural heritage in many regions of the world, the Commission on Intangible Cultural Heritage began its work with consultations with anthropologists in many different countries. A first Research Planning Meeting was also held at the *Regional Center for Multidisciplinary Research* (CRIM) of the *National University of Mexico* (UNAM) in Cuernavaca, Mexico on 24–28 February 2012. This report summarizes the key discussions and issues raised during that meeting, which were further developed in the papers presented by the participants.

L. Arizpe and C. Amescua (eds.), *Anthropological Perspectives on Intangible Cultural Heritage*, SpringerBriefs in Environment, Security, Development and Peace 6, DOI: 10.1007/978-3-319-00855-4, © The Author(s) 2013

A.1 The Need for Reflexivity in Intangible Cultural Heritage Research

Scientific research into intangible cultural heritage has a long history in anthropology and other related social sciences, although its concepts have evolved greatly in the last three decades. Working on the normative and juridical aspects of the *Convention on Intangible Cultural Heritage*, anthropologists, legal professionals and political scientists have developed innovative concepts and methods in this interdisciplinary field. At the same time, many anthropologists have worked on the operational guidelines of the Convention, with a special focus on the organization and impact of national and micro-regional programmes on intangible cultural heritage. They have primarily dealt with localities, cultural holders, practitioners, communities and related stakeholders. Also, they have closely collaborated with non-governmental organizations and emerging local associations working on intangible cultural heritage projects.

At present, there is a need to bring together researchers involved in different levels of investigation. Diversity of conceptual and methodological approaches must be addressed; this involves ethnographic as well as rapid assessment techniques. Also, the ways in which experts and community practitioners of intangible cultural heritage interact and may become involved is crucial in order to understand distinct impacts in varying countries and settings. There is a need to broaden the field of research into intangible cultural heritage to cover the multiplicity of cultural practices and styles of performance while constructing a common outlook on intangible cultural heritage research.

The range of perspectives that have rapidly evolved in the social sciences during the last decades, influenced by critical theory, cultural studies and interpretive approaches, has distanced investigations in the field of intangible cultural heritage from mainstream research in the social sciences, especially in anthropology. The new ways of managing cultures and analysing cultural processes per se require deeper dialogue and collaborative research.

A.2 General Issues in Intangible Cultural Heritage Research

Anthropological studies and fieldwork on intangible cultural heritage display a great divergence of interests, aims and purposes in understanding and implementing projects in this field. In some instances, anthropological knowledge is being used for cultural politics in ways that undermine the objectives of scientific research and, in the long term, make it more difficult to attain the goals of the UNESCO Convention on Intangible Cultural Heritage. At the same time, it is precisely the outcomes of such policy-oriented programmes (including inventories) that must be analysed to better define and categorize the production of intangible cultural heritage. Indeed, to develop more precise knowledge about intangible cultural heritage it is necessary to destabilize several key concepts. Therefore, the participants at the Research Planning Meeting identified these key issues:

Heritage

- 'Heritage' is a value-laden concept with no neutral ground of connotation. It is also part of a mode of cultural production.
- Heritage is about the regulation and negotiation of the multiplicity of meanings of the past, and about the arbitration or mediation of the cultural and social politics of identity, belonging and exclusion.
- Heritage emerges from the nexus of politics and power: it is a project of symbolic domination as well.
- Heritage articulates relations of power and relations of meaning, that is, it is defined within a process of the social production of meaning.
- Heritage, as a normative concept, entails evaluation. In comparison with tangible heritage, intangible cultural heritage appears to be not as substantial and enduring, and hence of less obvious value.

Intangibility and Hybridity

- Intangibility affords cultural creations an uncanny ability to travel—in fact, such creations tend to be things like languages that cannot be left behind, although they may, over time, transform or be forgotten.
- Anthropology has studied hybridity as well as the intermingling of cultural practices in many societies. The intrinsic nature of cultural exchange is difficult to manage in cultural politics and in policy-oriented intangible cultural heritage programmes. New definitions and criteria are required to clearly identify intangible cultural heritage practices.
- Pluricultural heritage practices may lead both to convergence and to conflict, and they demonstrate that people are attracted by such practices for different reasons.

The Tangible and the Intangible

- All heritage is intangible: as an ascribed value it always has a social impact.
- Intangible heritage must have a material dimension: the processes involved assume materiality and tangibility.
- Furthermore, there is the intangible within the intangible, that is, the symbolic dimension of intangible cultural heritage.

The Dynamics of Cultural Choice

- Safeguarding entails a politics of inclusion and of exclusion. This may have an impact in the village or on regional forms of management of intangible cultural heritage.
- In safeguarding intangible cultural heritage, different groups within a community of practitioners may want to either preserve or discard particular manifestations of cultural heritage. In this dynamic of preservation and adaptation, research may be useful in understanding the cultural claims of gatekeepers, practitioners and stakeholders.
- Adopting new elements or conserving traditional 'integrity' often ranges conservators against innovators. How far may new forms of performance or innovation be pursued without altering the core conception of a given cultural practice?
- Divergence and discrepancy occur when some social actors are given pre-eminence while others are disengaged in programmes and projects to safeguard intangible cultural heritage.
- A different kind of cultural dynamics occurs when programmes give priority to preserving cultural practices rather than to strengthening the social practices in which they are embedded (Photo A1).

Photo A1 Research Planning Meeting on Intangible Cultural Heritage, CRIM–UNAM, Cuernavaca, Morelos (2012). *Source* Photo by Carolina Buenrostro

Representation

- Research is needed into intangible cultural heritage understood as people's 'representations', as their 'representation of themselves', and as 'representations of representations of representations', that is, as performances of a narrative which is itself a constructed discourse on the production of a historical or social event. Safeguarding may then become a device to dress historic cultural elements with patrimonial value.
- Cultural elements may officially be 'patrimonialized', which implies a staging of heritage. Can these representations shift from an axis of authenticity or counterfeit to an articulation of verisimilitude and pure fantasy?
- In the politics of representation itself there are questions as to who represents whom and why: leaders of practitioners, community leaders, governments or state authorities. This includes those who speak for women or men, or for different generations.
- Public representation: how is intangible cultural heritage given a public representation in the way communities wish to present themselves and what is missing in such public representations?
- Intangible cultural heritage must then be understood as an arena of social and symbolic representations with an intrinsic bi-dimensionality:
  - representational and practical
  - symbolic and expressive
  - phenomenological and living expression (Photo A2).

Photo A2 Research Planning Meeting on Intangible Cultural Heritage, CRIM–UNAM, Cuernavaca, Morelos (2012). *Source* Photo by Carolina Buenrostro

Mediation in the Safeguarding Process

- Communication between public agents and social actors is never fully satisfactory: it is based on incomplete knowledge, problematic assumptions and doubtful interpretations.
- The importance of community agency in the decision-making process is related to safeguarding—but are the terms and implications of the negotiations clearly understood by everyone?
- Categories and procedures in legal instruments may not have equivalents in customary concepts and practices. This is a major issue that must be taken up in the procedures of inscription of intangible cultural heritage in the Representative List, in the Urgent Safeguarding List, and in national inventories.
- Finding the mediations is important to exploring the workings of cultural transmission: the need to track protagonists, institutions, gestures, interactions, places, ideologies, critical moments, smells, texts, silences, ordinary moments, sounds, emotions, objects and technologies. The whole concept of cultural transmission, in fact, becomes critical when all such aspects are analysed.
- Mediation is not a power-free enterprise/activity and its consequences must be accounted for.

Archaeology of Intangible Cultural Heritage

- Intangible cultural heritage implies identity, a sense of social and affective appropriation, production of historical meaning for a social group, the concept of the 'inherited' (legacy) that must be transmitted in order to build a link between past and future.
- As in culture, research must address the issue of practices or forms of knowledge that are no longer being reproduced, or that are endangered, and identify the reasons for and dynamics of such changes.
- Anthropologists should focus on recording rituals, stories, oratory, songs, etc.— in all cases, to record the archive and repertoire. Conversion of the intangible into tangible materializations (recordings, transcriptions, grammars) implies a transition from live and evolving transmission to 'dead', non-evolving transmission. Two processes become crucial:

  – revitalization and
  – refunctionalization (hybrid transmission).

- Visual documentation of intangible cultural heritage: visual documentation only represents a portion of reality, which has been separated with a specific intention. Nevertheless, visual documentation is a tool that may capture intangible cultural heritage manifested through the body; it is also a means to transmit a specific heritage to posterity; or it can even be a 'recovery point' for future generations, in case the heritage is not passed on. Documentation processes might serve different purposes such as record retention, transmission or training of successors, or publicity and dissemination.

Cultural Transmission

- To better grasp the working of cultural transmission it is necessary to distinguish between two levels of analysis: what can be called the 'reflexive theory of transmission' (the way people perceive and verbalize the process of transmission and its loss) and the observable 'processes of transmission' through which knowledge, emotions, and practices are *actually* transferred.
- In some cases, UNESCO's project of safeguarding does not correspond to the way cultural transmission and loss are conceived by locals. In others, culture holders speak about permanence and loss in ways that do not match the sense expressed by international experts.
- Concepts, practices and emotions from the past do not suddenly 'happen' in people, they entail a long process where they circulate among generations and peers, being appropriated by individuals and groups who *actively* acquire and transform them.
- The distinction between explicit transmission and implicit transmission must be addressed, even as it occurs in the seemingly least significant events of everyday life.
- The scene of cultural transmission is historical and it is not linear: it may resituate the chain of transmission in the midst of such historical contingencies.
- Transmission and reproduction:

    - Analyse the role of educators in school systems in the transmission of intangible cultural heritage. Point to visible contradictions among different repertoires of transmission.
    - Pair transmission and loss (voluntary or involuntary): the opposite of transmission would be 'non-transmission'. Anthropologists should document non-transmission but also reflect on why it takes place.
    - Analyse the processes of transmission of intangible cultural heritage from rural settings to urban areas.

- Cultural transmission is a global issue now (Photo A3).

Photo A3 Research Planning Meeting on Intangible Cultural Heritage, CRIM–UNAM, Cuernavaca, Morelos (2012). *Source* Photo by Carolina Buenrostro

Linguistics and Intangible Cultural Heritage

- Linguistic relativism, in certain contexts, adds a theoretical perspective that may offer a better understanding of cultural and linguistic diversity. It entails the following points:
  - Words must be understood not as labels but as processes of categorization.
  - The semantic fields that constitute each culture vary from one culture to another.
  - Through the understanding of semantic fields, ethnoscience builds different models of representation.
  - Who plays a role in preserving endangered languages and who does not? Here gender and age differences, among others, should be identified and made visible.
- The linguistic paradigm suggests a focus not on the cultural creation itself but on the expertise involved, and the ways that expertise is transmitted or reproduced over time.
- Language acquisition requires five things: time, effort, motivation, input, and opportunities for use. Literacy requires a sixth, instruction. In the case of intangible cultural heritage, a seventh must be added: meaningfulness.
- Include transmission arrangements in descriptions of intangible cultural heritage's practices and manifestations: information on how they are

transmitted, through which relationships, and on institutions, pedagogical practices, and value structures.

Diversity and Authenticity

- Authenticity is a well-known issue in cultural heritage. Dealing with it in intangible cultural heritage at the practical level requires recognizing and addressing several types of claims.
- One of the central contradictions of modernity is the simultaneity of a diffusionist spirit (tendencies to homogenization) and the acute need to preserve otherness (diversity).
- When thinking about intangible cultural heritage, using the framework of diversity might be very productive: analyse constellations of cultural expressions or practices instead of single events.
- It is important to think about who are the 'others' of authenticity. Is authenticity opposed to hybridity? Is it opposed to simulation? Who builds which oppositions?
- Authenticity appears as a 'non-issue' in the academic and international policy arenas, but at the local level it is still a relevant question for practitioners and stakeholders.

Levels of Analysis

- Intangible cultural heritage 'from above' refers to the shaping of heritage regimes. What kinds of heritage regimes are being shaped? What particular concerns are fuelling these heritage regimes? Heritage conceptualization comprises negative emotions and painful experiences. Destruction and loss are constitutive of the very notion of heritage. The fundamentalist ideology behind heritage preservation derives from the modernist obsession with loss. Therefore, curative concerns can be identified behind the notion of heritage.
- Intangible cultural heritage 'from below' refers to communities, practitioners, stakeholders. In contrast, political and administrative decisions at the international level have direct effects on human lives globally. Nevertheless, heritage groups and intangible cultural heritage bearers and practitioners are not passive receivers of cultural politics but actors who make choices in negotiating, transforming or rejecting available options; they are active 'subjects' who analyse their own world, culture and society, subjects with a view and a voice over what matters for them. Several issues arise from this perspective:
  - *Agency*: Which kind of 'agencies' are built or involved in the creation, reproduction and management of intangible cultural heritage? Communities are not homogenous entities; constant negotiations are undertaken amongst

internally diverse groups. Therefore it is important to analyse the dynamics of consensus building within heterogeneity. How communities negotiate memory and identity points to heritage within themselves and with others.

- *Ownership*: This might be one of the most complex issues when thinking about intangible cultural heritage at the local level, in constant interaction with global forces. It is crucial that communities establish their own mechanisms to deal with ownership when their intangible cultural heritage leaves their communities through official inventory mechanisms, media, academic research, etc. But there are less evident issues regarding ownership within communities. There is an intrinsic relationship between ownership and socially accepted practices. The moral foundation of ownership depends on the person in question belonging to the social group and thus having legitimate access to the source of knowledge and its symbolic meanings.

- *Shifting loyalties:* What happens with intangible cultural heritage in contexts of cultural proximity, hybridity and diasporas, where loyalties are not bound to a single community or group? How are intellectual property rights assigned to specific groups in those contexts? Is there a formal or informal recognition of the intangible cultural heritage of permanent diasporas in host communities? Will incorporation (acceptance) of the recombined cultural heritage of native and migrant groups gain acceptance as part of the native cultural tradition? In these changing contexts tradition can creatively meet with innovation through multi-sited and multi-situated experiences.

- Go beyond deconstruction to empirically confirm arguments such as heritage as the capture of evolving cultural contents; the original substantive purpose of heritage including dynamics of inclusion and exclusion of owners or carriers.
- Question the relations between place, intangible heritage, social activities and the politics of conservation. What are the conflicts? The notion of cultural spaces or cultural places is very controversial, since it may oppose the interests or claims of companies and governments for particular territories.

A.3   Specific Intangible Cultural Heritage Research Issues and Themes

During the meeting there was a clear consensus that anthropology, and the social sciences in general, may significantly contribute to a better understanding of intangible cultural heritage both conceptually and normatively, but also in terms of the processes that are involved in the creation, transmission, reproduction and even loss of intangible cultural heritage. Among such processes are:

- Decision-making and categorization
- Ownership of conflicts and abuses
- Conflicting values and claims
- Ethnography of heritage institutions.

A.4 Intersecting Paths of Analysis

- An empirical standpoint may help researchers to reflect on the effects that were created by intervention and inclusion in the Lists at the community level. Is there a shift in ontological status? Or is there rather an epistemological shift? But it may also be useful both for refining the classificatory grid for intangible cultural heritage lists and inventories and for imagining viable alternatives to the problematic procedure of cataloguing living heritage.
- Relationship between social movements and heritage: how is intangible cultural heritage understood and resignified in the context of social movements?
- Heritage relates to biocultural diversity. Intangible cultural heritage research may be understood as a way of building alternatives to challenges posed by a political geoecology: by beliefs and a ritualization of the relationship of human groups to their natural environment. It may refer to the ways global environmental change is addressed at the local level through 'adjustment rituals', environmental management through ethnic and traditional knowledge, and ethnocultural technologies.
- Intangible cultural heritage, mobility and contact zones: political borders or borderline contexts in migration. The dynamics of intangible cultural heritage in the case of diasporas, transnational communities and immigrant groups are an important field of research.
- Intangible cultural heritage and virtual communities: does the use of information and communication technologies (or new media) impact on intangible cultural heritage?

A.5 Intangible Cultural Heritage and Cultural Issues

- The hidden face of the destructive dimension of cultures, for example forms of symbolic destruction and gendered destructive practices.
- Understanding global regimes through the study of intangible cultural heritage institutions.
- Reflection on the processes of innovation, as heritage is inscribed in the dynamics of extra-communitarian, micro-regional, national and global transformation, for instance indigenous art in the global sphere.

A.6 Methodological Issues

- Ethnographic experience may be very useful as a means to address structural difficulties and challenges in the implementation of the Convention; to evaluate the impacts of the Lists, for example, when the proposals for the Representative

List are selected without taking into account local communities; or when
inscriptions create conflicts within communities—collateral effects among
different communities of practitioners.

- Development of methods to analyse the local understanding of concepts used
  globally or institutionally, such as heritage, creation, ownership, knowledge,
  authenticity or symbolic commonalities.
- Establishing hard facts in order to comparatively measure change and variation
  in cultural practices, both between different historical periods and
  synchronically.

A.7 Contributions of Social Science and Anthropology to a Better Implementation of the Convention from a Critical Perspective

Strengthening communication and networking among social scientists,
intellectuals and knowledge bearers must be a priority if new paths for research
and policy improvements are to be brought into the work of the Convention on
Intangible Cultural Heritage. A dialogue between scholars and authorities at the
international, national and local levels is strongly needed both to favour a better
implementation of the Convention and to identify conflicting interests, languages
and world views that might hinder its practical functioning. This should be done
without ignoring the fact that scientific research tends to be streamlined by
political bodies and by those in charge of programmes responsible for the
implementation of the Convention.

- Inventories and lists entail problems such as setting in stone boundaries and
  definitions of what in reality is a fluid, dynamic and constantly evolving process;
  they presume a process of detachment and fragmentation of cultural phenomena
  into manageable units, producing the reification of culture. It is a culturally
  biased practice that highlights some cultural elements and understates others.
  These are not new concerns; they have been raised by scholars throughout the
  years. There is a need to think about alternative forms of registering and
  inventorying.

Anthropology can also contribute to an analysis of procedures and relationships
involving realpolitik, political power and prestige, economic gains, and the
flourishing of intermediaries of several kinds in the selection of candidatures for
the List.

Overall, as has been established, the social sciences and anthropology provide
important contributions and a rich potential for work on intangible cultural
heritage at all levels, paving the way for significant and innovative future
developments.

Commission on Intangible Cultural Heritage

In the past 15 years, the convergence of anthropological interest in rapid cultural change and traditions and the concern of social agents about the loss and transformation of living cultural heritage have led to very valuable outcomes. In the 1966 Report of the United Nations Commission on Culture and Development "Our Creative Diversity", in which many anthropologists were involved, including Chie Nakane, Marshall Sahlins and Lourdes Arizpe (who was head of the Secretariat for the Commission), anthropological research was the basis for proposing a set of international development guidelines regarding indigenous cultures, cultural pluralism and the preservation of cultural heritage.

At present, the organizing bodies and the NGO network of the 2003 International Convention of Intangible Cultural Heritage have been actively consolidating the normative and organizational aspects in several meetings held in Paris and Abu Dhabi. However, the theoretical and methodological aspects of defining, registering and systematizing research in this field have not advanced at the same pace. Therefore, at the recent General Assembly of the State Parties to the 2003 Convention, held in June 2010 at Unesco (Paris), the normative documents of the Convention were amended, calling for closer collaboration with the scientific research community on intangible cultural heritage.

The IUAES–ISSC Commission on Intangible Cultural Heritage aims to provide the scientific and intellectual arena for anthropologists and ethnologists who have the fieldwork knowledge of and analytical tools for living cultural heritage to provide in-depth analyses of cultural groups in very diverse geographical regions.

Chairperson:
Prof. Lourdes Arizpe – National Autonomous University of Mexico

Vice-Chairs:
Prof. Kristin Kuutma – University of Estonia
Prof. Antonio Arantes – University of Campinas (Brazil)

Secretary:
Prof. Cristina Amescua – National Autonomous University of Mexico
Website: <http://www.iuaes.org/comm/heritage.html>.

L. Arizpe and C. Amescua (eds.), *Anthropological Perspectives on Intangible Cultural Heritage*, SpringerBriefs in Environment, Security, Development and Peace 6, DOI: 10.1007/978-3-319-00855-4, © The Author(s) 2013

Centro Regional de Investigaciones Multidisciplinarias

The Regional Center for Multidisciplinary Research (CRIM) is an academic institution ascribed to the Coordination of Humanities at the National Autonomous University of Mexico (UNAM). It is located in the City of Cuernavaca on the Morelos Campus of UNAM. Its objectives are:

1. Focus on multidisciplinary research in social sciences, humanities and other disciplines, mostly aimed at tackling specific problems at the local, regional, national and international levels, and their implications within globalization processes.
2. Contribute to the creation of knowledge in relevant and innovative arenas addressing social problems that require the convergence of different disciplines for their study.
3. Contribute to the development of a multidisciplinary approach to humanities, and focus on the development of innovative theoretical and methodological perspectives.
4. Participate in educational programs so as to contribute to the academic training of professionals in social sciences, humanities and other disciplines.
5. Disseminate by all possible means the results of CRIM's research projects. Website: <http://www.crim.unam.mx>.

L. Arizpe and C. Amescua (eds.), *Anthropological Perspectives on Intangible Cultural Heritage*, SpringerBriefs in Environment, Security, Development and Peace 6, DOI: 10.1007/978-3-319-00855-4, © The Author(s) 2013

Universidad Nacional Autonoma de Mexico

The National Autonomous University of Mexico (UNAM) was founded on 21 September 1551 under the name 'Royal and Pontifical University of Mexico'. It is the biggest and most important university in Mexico and in Ibero-America.

As part of the *Centennial Celebrations of Mexican Independence*, the National University was officially created on 22 September 1919. With the intention of widening educational opportunities in the country, the effort to launch the National University, though often hampered by adversity, was initially spearheaded by Congressman Justo Sierra in 1881. His vision finally materialized in 1910 with the inauguration of the *National University of Mexico* at a ceremony held in the National Preparatory School Amphitheatre, where as Secretary of Public Instruction, Sierra told the audience that the thrust of the National University's educational project was to concentrate, systematize and disseminate knowledge in order to prepare the Mexican people for the future. One hundred years after the creation of the University, Justo Sierra's inaugural address still rings true: (...) *we are telling the university community today that truth is unfolding: go seek it (...) you have been charged with the realization of a political and social ideal which can be summed up thus: democracy and liberty.*

The fundamental aim of UNAM is to serve both the country and humanity, to train professionals, to organize and carry out research, mainly on national problems and conditions, and to offer cultural benefits in the broadest sense possible.

Website: <www.unam.mx>.

L. Arizpe and C. Amescua (eds.), *Anthropological Perspectives on Intangible Cultural Heritage*, SpringerBriefs in Environment, Security, Development and Peace 6, DOI: 10.1007/978-3-319-00855-4, © The Author(s) 2013

Editors Biographies

Lourdes Arizpe is a professor at the Regional Center for Multidisciplinary Research of the National University of Mexico. She received an MA from the National School of History and Anthropology in Mexico in 1970 and a PhD in Anthropology from the London School of Economics and Political Science, UK, in 1975. She has pioneered anthropological studies on migration, gender, rural development, and global change and culture in Mexico, in Latin America, and in international research groups, both academic and policy-oriented. Professor Arizpe taught at Rutgers University through a Fulbright grant in 1979 and carried out research in India and Senegal with a John F. Guggenheim grant in 1981. She was director of the National Museum of Popular Cultures in Mexico 1985–1988. She was elected President of the National Association of Ethnologists of Mexico in 1986 and Secretary to the Mexican Science Academy in 1992. Professor Arizpe was Director of the Institute of Anthropological Studies at the National University of Mexico, was elected President of the International Union of Anthropological and Ethnological Sciences in 1988, and successfully organized its World Congress in Mexico in 1993.

Lourdes Arizpe became a member of the United Nations Commission on Culture and Development, and soon afterwards was designated Assistant Director General for Culture at UNESCO 1994–98. She was elected President of the International Social Science Council for 2004–2008, and participated as a member of the Academic Faculty of the Global Economic Forum at Davos, Switzerland 2000–2004. At the United Nations Institute for Research on Social Development, she was Chair of the Board 2005–2011 and a member of the Committee for Development Policy of the Economic and Social Council. She is a member of the Board of Trustees of the Library of Alexandria in Egypt.

L. Arizpe and C. Amescua (eds.), *Anthropological Perspectives on Intangible Cultural Heritage*, SpringerBriefs in Environment, Security, Development and Peace 6, DOI: 10.1007/978-3-319-00855-4, © The Author(s) 2013

Lourdes Arizpe became an Honorary Member of the Royal Anthropological Institute of the UK in 1995, and has received the Order of "Palmes Académiques" from France in 2007, the Award for Academic Merit of the Universidad Veracruzana in Mexico, and an Honorary Doctorate from the University of Florida at Gainesville in 2010.

Cristina Amescua holds a PhD in Social Anthropology from the National Autonomous University of Mexico, and is a member of the faculty of the National University of Mexico's Regional Center for Multidisciplinary Research as a professor and researcher. In recent years she has conducted research in the following fields: Migration and Culture; Intangible Cultural Heritage; Anthropology of Violence; and Migration and Climate Change. She serves as Executive Director for the UNESCO Chair on Intangible Heritage and Cultural Diversity and as Secretary of the IUAES/ISSC Commission for Research on Intangible Cultural Heritage. In 2013, her doctoral dissertation was awarded the best doctoral thesis by UNAM's Research Center on North America. She has published more than ten chapters in books, and is currently co-editing the collective books *Intangible Cultural Heritage: Safeguarding Experiences* and *Politics in Movement: State, Culture, Citizenship and Exile*. Some of her publications include *Culture and Migration. Intangible Cultural heritage en contact zones: a struggle for authenticity or an option for conviviality* (UIA, 2010), and *Regional Analysis of Proclamations of Masterpieces of Oral and Intangible Heritage of Humanity* (CRIM–UNAM, 2011). She also collaborated on UNESCO's World Report: *Investing in Cultural Diversity and Intercultural Dialogue* (2009).

Biographies of the Contributors

Amescua, Cristina has a Doctoral degree from the *National Autonomous University of Mexico* (UNAM). She currently works as a researcher and professor at the Regional Center for Multidisciplinary Research (UNAM). She is Executive Director of the Unesco Unitwin Chair on Intangible Cultural Heritage and Cultural Diversity. She has collaborated with international organizations such as UNESCO, the *International Social Sciences Council* (ISSC) and the *International Research Centre for Intangible Cultural Heritage in The Regions of Asia and the Pacific* (IRCI). Her current research focuses on migration and intangible cultural heritage.
Address: Centro Regional de Investigaciones Multidisciplinarias—UNAM, Av Universidad s/n Circuito II, campus UAEM, Col. Chamilpa, CP 62210 Cuernavaca, Morelos, México.
Email: <cristina.amescua@correo.crim.unam.mx>.
Website: <www.crim.unam.mx>

Arantes, Antonio has a Doctoral degree from Cambridge University (1978) and was one of the founders of the Anthropology Department at the State University of Campinas (UNICAMP), Brazil, in 1968, where he still works as a researcher and professor of anthropology. He was president of the Brazilian Anthropological Association and Secretary General of the Latin-American Anthropological Association. He has been president of the *National Institute of Historic and Artistic Heritage of Brazil* (IPHAN). He is a public policy consultant specializing in cultural heritage.
Address: Universidade Estadual de Campinas. Rua Cora Coralina s/n—Cidade Universitária, "Zeferino Vaz", Barão Geraldo, 13081-970—Campinas, SP—Brasil—Caixa-postal: 6110.
Email: <antonio_arantes@terra.com.br>.
Website: <www.unicamp.br>.

Arizpe, Lourdes is a professor at the National University of Mexico, has a PhD in anthropology from the London School of Economics and Political Science and an Honorary Doctorate from the University of Florida. She pioneered anthropological studies on migration, gender, rural development, global change and culture in Mexico and Latin America and carried out research in India and Senegal with a John F. Guggenheim grant. While Director of the Institute of Anthropological Studies at the National University of Mexico, she became President of the International Union of Anthropological and Ethnological Sciences. She was a member of the United Nations Commission on Culture and Development and soon afterwards Assistant Director General for Culture at UNESCO (1994–98). She was elected President of the International Social Science Council for 2004–2008 and participated as a member of the Academic Faculty of the Global Economic Forum at Davos, Switzerland. She is a member of the Board of Trustees of the Library of Alexandria in Egypt. Lourdes Arizpe has received the Order of Academic Palms from France in 2007, the Award for Academic Merit of the Universidad Veracruzana, and an Honorary Doctorate from the University of Florida in 2010. *Address*: Centro Regional de Investigaciones Multidisciplinarias—UNAM, Av Universidad s/n Circuito II, campus UAEM, Col. Chamilpa, CP 62210 Cuernavaca, Morelos, México.
Email: <la2012@correo.crim.unam.mx>.
Website: <www.crim.unam.mx>.

Berliner, David is an Associate Professor of Anthropology at Université Libre de Bruxelles, and the co-editor of Social Anthropology/Anthropologie Sociale. He has conducted ethnographic research in Guinea-Conakry, Burkina Faso, Gabon and Laos. His areas of theoretical expertise include the anthropology of cultural heritage and social memory as well as the study of gender and sexuality. Some of his articles have been published in American Ethnologist, Cahiers d'Études Africaines, JRAI, Terrain, L'Homme, RES anthropology, and Aesthetics and Anthropological Quarterly.
Address: Laboratoire d'Anthropologie des Mondes Contemporains, ULB-Institut de sociologie, Avenue Jeanne, 44 - CP124 - B-1050 Bruxelles.
Email: <David.Berliner@ulb.ac.be>.
Website: <http://lamc.ulb.ac.be/spip.php?article114&lang=en>.

Kuutma, Kristin has a Doctoral degree from the University of Washington in 2002, when she also became a faculty member of the University of Tartu (Estonia), where she still teaches, among others, cultural research and ethnology courses. In 2003 she was awarded the Annual Award of the Estonian Cultural Foundation for her research analysis and overview of the Estonian, Latvian and Lithuanian song and dance festivals, and of the Kihnu cultural space, proclaimed UNESCO Masterpieces of Oral and Intangible Heritage. From 2006 to 2010 she was Estonia's representative to the UNESCO Intergovernmental Committee for the

Safeguarding of the Intangible Cultural Heritage, where she served as Vice-Chair from 2006 to 2007. Kristin Kuutma is Professor of Cultural Research at the University of Tartu, Estonia. Her research focuses on cultural history and anthropology, heritage studies, policy and representation. She is the head of the UT programme of the Graduate School of Culture Studies and Arts, and chairs the Estonian National Commission for Unesco.
Address: Ülikooli 16-211, Tartu, Estonia.
Email: <kristin.kuutma@ut.ee>.
Website: <http://www.ut.ee/en>.

Machuca R., Jesús Antonio is a Sociologist from the Faculty of Political and Social Sciences at the National Autonomous University of Mexico. He is a researcher at the Directorate of Ethnology and Social Anthropology of the National Institute of Anthropology and History (DEAS-INAH). He has had an active role in the implementation of the UNESCO 2003 Convention for the Safeguarding of Intangible Cultural Heritage in Mexico and has attended several meetings of experts at UNESCO. He is currently coordinating the INAH Seminars (1) Cultural Heritage in the Twenty-first Century, and (2) Interdisciplinary Approaches to Memory Studies. His research focuses on the scope of cultural heritage's transformations in the context of globalization.
Address: Av. San Jerónimo núm. 880, Col. San Jerónimo Lídice, Delegación Magdalena Contreras C.P. 10200, México, D.F.
Email: <machucaantonio@hotmail.com>.
Website: <http://deas.inah.gob.mx>.

Miyata, Shigeyuki has a Master of Arts from WASEDA University. Currently, he is a director in the Department of Intangible Cultural Heritage at the National Research Institute for Cultural Properties, Tokyo (NRICPT). He is a member of the world heritage and intangible cultural heritage committee at the Advisory councils in the agency for cultural affairs, Japan.
Address: NRICPT, 13-43, Ueno Park, Taito-ku, Tokyo, 110-8713, Japan.
Email: <miyata@tobunken.go.jp>.
Website: <www.tobunken.go.jp>.

Pratt, Mary Louise is Silver Professor in the Department of Social and Cultural Analysis and the Department of Spanish and Portuguese at New York University, where she teaches courses in cultural theory and in Latin American literature and thought. Formerly Olive H. Palmer Professor of Humanities at Stanford University, she held a Catedra Patrimonial at CIESAS-Guadalajara in 1998–99, and was president and vice president of the Modern Language Association from 2002 to 2005.

Address: Department of Spanish and Portuguese, New York University, 19
University Place, New York, NY 10003.
Email: <mlp7@nyu.edu>.
Website: <http://sca.as.nyu.edu/object/marypratt.html>.

Rosaldo, Renato is Lucie Stern Professor in the Social Sciences at New York
University where he has taught courses in Anthropology and Social and Cultural
Analysis. His publications include *Cultural Citizenship in Island Southeast Asia
Nation and Belonging in the Hinterlands (Editor,* 2003); *Anthropology of
Globalization: A Reader* (with Jon Inda, editors, 2001); *Culture and Truth: The
Remaking of Social Analysis* (1989); *Ilongot Headhunting. 1883–1974: A Study in
Society and History (1980).* He has a great interest in poetry and creative writing.
Address:
Email: <renato.rosaldo@nyu.edu>.
Website: <http://anthropology.as.nyu.edu/object/RenatoRosaldo.html>.

On This Book

A decade after the approval of the UNESCO 2003 Convention for the Safeguarding of Intangible Cultural Heritage (ICH), the concept has gained wide acceptance at local, national and international levels. Communities are recognizing and celebrating their Intangible Heritage; governments are devoting important efforts to the construction of national inventories; anthropologists and professionals from different disciplines are building a new field of study. The ten chapters of this book include the peer-reviewed papers of the First Planning Meeting of the International Social Science Council's Commission on Research on ICH held at the Centro Regional de Investigaciones Multidisciplinarias (UNAM) in Cuernavaca, Mexico in 2012. The papers are based on fieldwork and direct involvement in assessing and reconceptualizing the outcomes of the UNESCO Convention. The report in the Annexe highlights the main points raised during the session.

L. Arizpe and C. Amescua (eds.), *Anthropological Perspectives on Intangible Cultural Heritage*, SpringerBriefs in Environment, Security, Development and Peace 6, DOI: 10.1007/978-3-319-00855-4, © The Author(s) 2013

CPSIA information can be obtained
at www.ICGtesting.com
Printed in the USA
LVOW02s1757160816

500630LV00003B/12/P